COACH K'S

LITTLE BLUE BOOK

COACH K'S
LITTLE BLUE BOOK

LESSONS FROM
COLLEGE BASKETBALL'S
BEST COACH

THE MESSAGE OF
MIKE KRZYZEWSKI
BY BARRY JACOBS

TOTAL
Sports
Illustrated

KINGSTON, NEW YORK   NEW YORK, NEW YORK

Published by
Total Sports Publishing
100 Enterprise Drive
Kingston, NY 12401

SPORTS ILLUSTRATED® and Total/SPORTS ILLUSTRATED are trademarks of Time Inc. Used under license.

For information about permission to reproduce selections from this book, please write to:
Permissions, Total Sports Publishing, 100 Enterprise Drive, Kingston, NY 12401
www.TotalSportsPublishing.com

Cover design: Mike Stromberg
Cover photograph: Bob Donnan
Interior design: Donna Harris
Photographs: Robert Crawford: 2-3, 8, 11, 12, 15, 16, 19, 21, 33, 36, 54, 79, 82, 85, 89, 97, 98, 106, 108, 126; Scott Cunningham, Georgia Tech: 59; Bob Donnan, Duke University: 48, 50, 73; Bob Donnan, North Carolina: 76, 103; Duke University: 22, 24, 28, 30, 31, 35, 38, 44, 46, 62, 64, 70, 77, 86, 90, 92, 95, 100, 114, 121, 123; Duke Sports Information: 80, 11, 113; Ned Hinshaw: 52; Bobby Hurley, Duke University: 66; Laettner, Duke University: 40; John McDonough, Duke University: 26; Hugh Morton: 72, 102; Hugh Morton, Duke University: 116; Hugh Morton, North Carolina: 67; North Carolina State: 94; Doug Pencincer, North Carolina: 58; Technical Photographic Services: 47, 118; University of North Carolina: 93

ISBN: 1-892129-26-4
Library of Congress Cataloging-in-Publication Data
Krzyzewski, Mike.
Coach K's little blue book : lessons from college basketball's best coach / edited by Barry Jacobs.
p. cm.
ISBN 1-892129-26-4
1. Krzyzewski, Mike. 2. Basketball coaches--United States--Biography.
3. Duke Blue Devils (Basketball team)--History. I. Jacobs, Barry. II. Title.
GV884.K79 A3 2000
796.323'092--dc21

Printed in Canada

DEDICATION

To Eddy Landreth and Ron Morris, friends in sports and beyond.

ACKNOWLEDGEMENTS

I've watched about 350 Duke games at Cameron Indoor Stadium, and seen the Blue Devils play another hundred times on the road. Cameron graces any game within its embrace, but recollections of specific games blur over the years. What lingers are impressions of individuals and teams, moments of drama and farce, memories of transcendent achievement and superior athleticism.

I've been around the Duke program with tape recorder and pad since the mid-1970s, and paid close attention from the time Mike Krzyzewski arrived on campus twenty years ago through the Blue Devils' latest run at a national title, ended by Florida in the 2000 Sweet 16.

Besides covering games and press conferences, each summer for most of those years I met Krzyzewski for at least an hour and recorded his thoughts on his team, the Atlantic Coast Conference, the characters and issues of the day, and sometimes even on himself. This book is largely based on those private interviews and public events, kindly facilitated by the staffs at the Duke basketball and sports information offices.

The Duke program is better than most about accommodating individual expression by players and assistant coaches. In that spirit Krzyzewski, who sets the tone, was most generous in sharing his time and thoughts.

A number of people transcribed tapes, including Dagmar Cooley, Anne Hastings, Susan Morris, Dan Pelletier, and John Royster. Most of the same folks, as well as Tony Britt and Rick Willenzik, assisted in collecting articles and compiling data that chronicle Krzyzewski's career and Duke's history with him as head coach.

For other assistance of various sorts I thank Dave Dewitt, Bernice Jacobs, Julian King, Gary Rosenthal, and the Moorefields dogs—Adams, Ford, Jefferson, Milly, Sparky, Ted, Truman, and Tyler—and cats—Crazy, Ego, and Raspberry.

Frank Daniels III and George Schlukbier of Total Sports first encouraged this project. John Thorn kept it viable and then worked with Kenneth Shouler, Donna Harris, Robert Crawford, and Beau Riffenburgh to bring it to fruition. Finally and always there's Robin, holding things together, soothing the savage beasts, and listening patiently to the chatter.

TABLE OF CONTENTS

INTRODUCTION

The exodus was pronounced and largely unexpected. Until the spring of 1999, Duke University basketball was immune to players leaving early for the pros, as if loyalty, tradition, and guilt held life's pecuniary forces at bay. Then, within weeks of one another, three underclassmen from a 37–2 squad declared for the NBA draft, led by Elton Brand, the national player of the year.

Awash in uncertainty, a trio of holdovers sought out their coach, Mike Krzyzewski (pronounced "shushefski"). Five years earlier Krzyzewski rushed recovery from back surgery, and his life nearly unraveled. This time, recuperating from hip replacement surgery, Krzyzewski stayed put for six weeks. So the veterans journeyed to Krzyzewski's house in the woods near Duke Forest "just to tell him the kingdom has not fallen," Shane Battier recalled.

Chris Carrawell said Krzyzewski was "elated to see us." Krzyzewski remembered crying when the veterans inquired: "Coach, we just want to know how you're doing. How are you doing?'"

Months later—after Duke repeated as the nation's top-ranked team and swept both the 2000 Atlantic Coast Conference regular season and tournament for the second consecutive year—the visit was cited as pivotal. Krzyzewski made it so. Ever attuned to leadership's call, he turned the emotion of the moment into a challenge to his players to believe all would be well within the Blue Devil universe.

"Coach, if you say so, I believe it," Carrawell declared.

And he did. Previously overshadowed, Carrawell enjoyed his best season in 2000. The versatile senior was ACC player of the year as Duke went 29–5, reached the NCAA Sweet 16, and reaffirmed its status as basketball's pre-eminent college program.

"He's definitely a great motivator, the best motivator in the game," Carrawell said of the fifty-three-year-old Krzyzewski. "He's a player's coach. A lot of coaches put limitations on you. He allows you to play, let your individual talent take over. He doesn't restrict your game, so to speak. So of course when you've got a coach who says: 'Go do it. Now, you've got to play defense, but go do it,' that gives you a hell of a lot of confidence."

Share this approach with a brimming handful of the nation's more gifted, team-oriented, and educationally qualified players; stir in resources, tradition, and a flexible, aggressive playing style; and infuse with Krzyzewski's passion, intelligence, and will. The result is an almost overpowering concoction.

The finish atop the polls in 2000 was Duke's fourth in the last fifteen years, and the first repeat No. 1 ranking by any program since 1981. The Blue Devils won at least twenty games for the fifteenth time during Krzyzewski's two-decade tenure, and their NCAA visit was their sixteenth in the past seventeen years.

"He's probably the coach of our generation," Jim Calhoun said before his Connecticut Huskies defeated Duke in the 1999 title game, Krzyzewski's eighth Final Four appearance and record fourth championship game defeat.

Krzyzewski is third all time in Final Four trips. But the 1999 visit was the first since Duke spiraled to 13–18 in 1995 while he was sidelined for two months recovering his health.

He returned from that experience chastened but undaunted, toughness intact, fires still burning fiercely if better controlled. "I can't tell you how confident I am when I look in his eyes on the bench and I see his intensity and I see him in the game, his support of us," senior guard Chris Collins said in 1996.

Mickie Krzyzewski (palms upraised), routinely sits above and behind the visiting bench in the upper deck of Cameron Indoor Stadium.

The next year Krzyzewski returned Duke to the top of the ACC standings, where it's remained ever since, its passionate, overplaying team defense setting a tempo of attack.

"That was the only alternative," said the coach, who shuns thoughts that divert from his purpose. "That was going to be the only way. If you want to get something done, you can't have a bunch of alternatives. You have to have absolutes."

The comeback has taken Krzyzewski's teams to new heights of efficiency. They've lost a mere 11 games against 98 victories over the past three seasons, an .899 winning percentage. Each of those years the Blue Devils led Division I in scoring.

At Cameron Indoor Stadium, their sixty-year-old campus arena, they were 42–2 from 1998 through 2000. On the road in the ACC, they were on a 19-game winning streak through the 2000 season.

Over the past two seasons the Devils posted a 66–7 record overall, a .904 winning percentage. That includes a 37–1 record in the ACC, fueled by a league-record 28 consecutive conference wins.

Duke's 37 victories in 1999 matched the most ever by a Division I team, a mark first set by the Blue Devils in 1986. Their scoring average in 1999 (91.8) was the ACC's highest in a quarter century, and their average winning margin (24.7 points) best in league history. Considered a near-unbeatable force, the 1999 Dukies reached the national championship game for the sixth time during Krzyzewski's tenure.

Krzyzewski came away with NCAA titles in 1991 and 1992,

The pregame ritual of bumping fists, here with Chris Carrawell, signifies that five fingers are stronger united than separate.

the only consecutive crowns since John Wooden's UCLA dynasty two decades earlier.

During a stretch from 1986 through 1994, Krzyzewski took seven of nine squads to the Final Four, including five straight from 1988–92. His .781 winning percentage in NCAA competition (50–14) is best among active coaches.

Despite playing routinely difficult schedules Krzyzewski has won better than three quarters of his games at Duke (498–160) and more overall than any two coaches in school history.

Defense led the way.

"Against a lot of systems you can pass the ball around and some player on the floor won't guard the ball as well as the others," Dave Bliss said after his Southern Methodist club lost to Duke in the 1988 NCAA Tournament. "It gives you a rest, an oasis. But there's no oasis against Duke. There's no place to put the ball where you know it's safe."

Since stumbling to consecutive losing records in 1982 and 1983, Krzyzewski's squads have won four of every five games

(460–113). During that stretch "Coach K" became a familiar figure, orchestrating teams with single-minded purpose, endlessly fascinated with the psychology of groups, leadership, and motivation.

"I personally think what he's done there is just as difficult as any run that anybody has ever had at any place, including Coach Wooden at UCLA," said Roy Williams, the highly successful Kansas coach. "The game is different now, it's more difficult now, more challenges, more parity in college basketball.

"Mike has not only taken them to the Final Four, not only won national championships, he's done it the right way. There's never any question that they're doing it the right way. He cares about the kids. There's nothing negative that you can say about the job that Mike has done."

That's not entirely true. There were surly early days with the media, a notorious run-in with Duke's student newspaper, times tinged with sanctimony, flirtations with the pros, defiance of doctor's orders that led to physical and emotional collapse, purging of long-loyal assistants after a last-place finish in his absence, and enough disgruntled players and academic exceptions to tarnish Krzyzewski's sterling image.

The flaws didn't prevent Krzyzewski from earning admiration and respect within sports and beyond. USA Today touted Duke back in 1992 as "The Perfect Program," an impression hardly changed since.

Krzyzewski claims not to be fooled. He remembers the difficult days, the 84–77 home defeat by lowly Wagner in 1983, the consecutive losing seasons, the second-guessing, the snubs by recruits, the sense of frustration, the uncertainty he could turn things around at Duke.

"What motivates me is losing," Krzyzewski confided after winning his second national title. "I still think of myself as a guy capable of going 10–17. Because I did that. And I was 11–17 the next year. So I know I've got to work my butt off. To me that's the motivation—I'm afraid. I don't want to lose the competitive edge I have right now. And the memory of what it was like to lose helps me."

That competitive edge was first honed in a Polish enclave in inner-city Chicago. Michael was the younger son of Polish immigrants Emily and Bill Krzyzewski. His father was an elevator operator, later a tavern owner, his mother a cleaning woman. Krzyzewski, a good athlete with a quick temper and an argumentative nature, soon recognized he was "really good" at basketball, and twice led Chicago's Catholic league in scoring.

The guard drew recruiting attention from Bobby Knight, coach at the U.S. Military Academy. Krzyzewski preferred a less strict school like Wisconsin or Creighton, but his parents were thrilled by the prospect of their son attending West Point.

He ultimately deferred to their wishes. "The family pride got me to do that. It was a great decision."

Attending the Academy, which Krzyzewski calls "a school for leaders", was tough. Playing for Knight was tougher. Toughest of all was Krzyzewski's senior season, when his father died and he captained the basketball squad, bearing the brunt of Knight's frequent verbal rampages.

But Krzyzewski handled it. During his three seasons from 1967–69 the Cadets were 51–23, twice led the nation in scoring defense, and twice reached the NIT, then a prestigious tournament. "He was a tough, aggressive-type player," recalled Bobby Cremins, the former South Carolina player and Georgia Tech coach.

Almost twenty years after the fact, Knight remembered a game against Bradley in which Krzyzewski got fouled by a poke in the eye. "It looked like it was hanging out of the socket," Knight said. "I knew he was looking backward out of that eye, but he made both free throws."

Krzyzewski graduated from West Point as a lieutenant in 1969, and on the same day married Carol "Mickie" Marsh. Stationed in the U.S. and South Korea, Krzyzewski rose to the rank of captain. Then he resigned

"Krzyzewskiville," a tent city erected by students waiting in line for entrance to key games, has strict rules of conduct and convenient internet access.

his commission to take a job as Knight's graduate assistant at Indiana in 1974–75, when the Hoosiers were 31–1 overall and undefeated in the Big Ten.

The next season, at age twenty-eight, Krzyzewski was hired as head coach at Army.

He coached at his alma mater from 1976–80, posting a 73–59 record. Taking over a program with three wins the year prior to his arrival, Krzyzewski directed the Cadets to a 20–8 record in 1977, his second season. The next year Army was 19–9 and invited to the NIT.

Krzyzewski's last Army team finished 9–17 even as Bill Foster left Duke for South Carolina after three consecutive NCAA bids and a trip to the 1978 national championship game. When Tom Butters, Duke's athletic director, sought Knight's suggestions for a replacement, Krzyzewski was among the former assistants the Indiana coach recommended.

"It was obvious to me that Mike's teams were well-coached, organized, intense competitors, and they played up to their abilities," recalled Steve Vacendak, who helped Butters research candidates. "That trademark was so obvious to those who saw Army play."

Butters toyed with pursuing aged Adolph Rupp, retired since 1972 as head coach of Kentucky. Ultimately he

Cameron Crazies, cultivated by Krzyzewski as his teams' "Sixth Man," at work.

considered the little-known Krzyzewski, Paul Webb of Old Dominion, Duke assistant Bob Wenzel, and another Knight protege, Mississippi's Bob Weltlich.

On their visit to Durham, North Carolina, as the Krzyzewskis strolled Duke's tree-lined, auto-restricted, Gothic campus, Mickie turned to her husband and said, "Don't screw this up." But not until the young couple left for the Raleigh-Durham airport to return home did Butters make up his mind.

"I had a list of things that are important to me in hiring anyone, and he met, in every way, all of those at the highest level," Butters said in 1990. "Everything he said made sense to me and the way in which he said it. The values he obviously had, all the credentials that he had—quite aside from basketball coaching—made sense to me."

At his introductory press conference in March 1980, Krzyzewski paid homage to Knight while asserting other influences, and promised man-to-man defense and an up-tempo, motion offense. Asked about his last name the new coach said, "It was a lot worse before I changed it."

The media immediately labeled Krzyzewski a "Bobby Knight disciple," an honorific with mixed connotations. Early on, the association proved damning as Krzyzewski sometimes came across as a self-described "goody two-shoes," other times as a prickly loser, raging at officials and touchy with the press.

Krzyzewski's first Duke team was 17–13, reaching the NIT. Then several holdovers graduated, big-name recruits flirted with Duke but went elsewhere, and the Blue Devils slid to

10–17. Just up the road, North Carolina won the 1982 national championship.

In dire need of talent, Krzyzewski brought in an acclaimed recruiting class for the 1982–83 season. But even with freshmen Mark Alarie, Jay Bilas, Johnny Dawkins, and David Henderson, the Devils struggled. As happened in 1982, Krzyzewski stuck with man-to-man defense almost exclusively, insisting that building proper habits was more important than using a zone to secure a few wins.

The 1983 record was 11–17, including the Wagner loss, a nadir for a program in a powerful league like the ACC. The season ended when Virginia, led by three-time national player of the year Ralph Sampson, beat Duke by 43 points in the ACC Tournament. To this day, that's the greatest margin of defeat in event history. Adding to the wound, in a maneuver Krzyzewski would later employ frequently, UVa's Terry Holland left his 7–4 star in the game until it was nearly over.

Meanwhile, down the road from Durham, Krzyzewski's contemporary, Jim Valvano, won the 1983 national title at N.C. State.

But Krzyzewski stuck with his sytem and Butters stuck with his coach, extending his contract in January 1984. By then the team was winning. Stabilized by the addition of Tommy Amaker, a freshman point guard, the Blue Devils opened the 1984 season with 14 victories in 15 games.

Duke eventually finished 24–10, upset North Carolina with Michael Jordan and Sam Perkins in the ACC Tournament, and earned its first NCAA Tournament appearance under Krzyzewski, the media's choice for ACC coach of the year.

Krzyzewski solidified his stature that season by denouncing what he called a "double standard" in league officiating that favored UNC's Dean Smith. League administrators detected no bias, but, afterward, referees did seem a bit more tolerant of Duke's very physical defense.

The 1985 season brought a 23–8 record and an NCAA visit that lasted two games. Then, with Dawkins leading the scoring, Amaker the defense and ballhandling, and everyone else filling multiple roles, the 1986 Blue Devils won 37 of 40 games and reached the NCAA title game. Along the way they captured Krzyzewski's first ACC title and first top ranking in the polls, and set a new NCAA record for victories in a season.

Krzyzewski considers the 1986 squad his best, given its experience, toughness, talent, and intelligence. Still, Louisville beat Duke, 72–69, in part because Amaker and Dawkins ran out of gas, and Krzyzewski, the national coach of the year, wouldn't risk using freshman guard Quin Snyder.

The next year every starter except Amaker graduated. "That was the most important season for me at Duke," Krzyzewski recalled.

But he'd begun winning recruiting wars with Dean Smith's UNC colossus, and now he turned to Danny Ferry, a versatile forward who'd spurned the Tar Heels. "To me, 1987 was the most difficult transition because it came right after the big year," Krzyzewski said. "That's when Danny had to step forward and be the key guy, and he was a sophomore."

Duke went 24–9, losing to Indiana and Knight in the Sweet 16. The next season the Blue Devils began a run of five straight Final Four appearances, capped by two NCAA titles.

Krzyzewski's program, reputation, and place in history were secured.

A staple of every season became Duke in the title hunt with talented players who graduate, speak articulately, and are difficult to stereotype on or off the court. Seasoned judgment in the post passed like a baton from Alarie to Ferry to Christian Laettner to Cherokee Parks, and at point from Amaker to Snyder to Bobby Hurley.

Under Krzyzewski's tutelage, Dawkins, Ferry, Laettner,

Hurley, Grant Hill, and Brand became consensus all-Americans. Cameron became a much-hyped shrine to edgy collegiate fanaticism within a classic setting.

Laettner's turnaround jumper to beat Kentucky in overtime, 104–103, in the 1992 East Regional final after catching a seventy-five-foot pass from Hill, took a place in basketball lore as the culminating play in one of the greatest games ever.

Meanwhile, we grew familiar with earnest Coach K—dark hair rarely out of place above his raptor-like visage—as the most visible embodiment of a university whose profile, contributions, and applicants soared during his tenure. Krzyzewski also emerged as a vocal lobbyist for men's basketball within NCAA circles, and as a well-paid spokesman for several corporations.

Not all went smoothly. Krzyzewski had a run-in with Duke's student newspaper, the *Chronicle*, in which he ambiguously invited ten reporters to the team locker room, then

Duke's motion offense has few set plays and plenty of flexibility.

blasted them profanely in front of squad and staff for an article one student wrote rating the Blue Devils.

After the season, Krzyzewski explored the possibility of coaching the Boston Celtics. But he returned to direct a volatile but gifted mix that added Hurley in 1990 and advanced to three straight national championship games. Duke finally won a title in 1991, following a stunning upset of undefeated Nevada-Las Vegas by defeating Kansas, 72–65.

The Dukies returned largely intact in 1992, though regular Billy McCaffrey and reserve Crawford Palmer transferred. Led by Laettner, the prickly and supremely competitive national player of the year, Duke went 34–2 and capped a second NCAA championship run with a 71–51 rout of Michigan and its Fab Five. There was talk of a Duke dynasty, and comparisons with Wooden's run at UCLA in the 1960s and early 70s.

Adjusting to life after Laettner, Duke was 24–8 in 1993 and lost in the Sweet 16. Krzyzewski found some solace in a multi-year contract with Nike, reportedly worth more than $6 million.

The 1994 squad was thin, but behind Hill the Blue Devils again reached the NCAA title game, falling to Arkansas, 76–72. The offseason saw renewed talk of Krzyzewski leaving for the pros, but he returned in 1995 and Duke got off to a 9–3 start.

Clearly, though, Krzyzewski hadn't recovered from October surgery to repair a ruptured disk in his back. "He looked like he was eighty years old," said Mickie Krzyzewski, who with her daughters had long maintained a presence on the program's periphery.

Suffering exhaustion and pain, Krzyzewski collapsed and was told by Butters to quit coaching for the season. "He just found out he doesn't change his clothes in a phone booth," said Dr. Mel Berlin, Duke's team physician.

Krzyzewski remained sidelined as Duke spiraled to a 13–18 mark and a last-place finish, then returned in March, vowing to better tend his health and priorities. Soon he canned several longtime aides, among them Pete Gaudet, who'd served as interim coach in his absence.

Krzyzewski is not one to hide his feelings, though he won't embarrass individual players in public.

Krzyzewski called an injury-decimated 1996 club a "bridge" to better times, and directed it to an 18-13 record and NCAA participation. More importantly, the defensive intensity returned, and with it Duke's confidence and identity.

By 1997, ball denial was back in vogue, and the Devils started a run in which they've finished first in the ACC, won at least two dozen games, and reached the NCAA Tournament for four straight years. With everyone back except Carrawell, and prep hotshot Chris Duhon coming aboard, they'll be favored to extend those streaks in 2001, and to contend for another NCAA title.

Krzyzewski, apparently content to tend his garden and his Blue Devils for the forseeable future, wouldn't have it any other way.

"He's coaching like he's defending the most precious thing in the world to him, and he does everything with the passion you would as if you were defending the most precious thing in the world to you," said Steve Wojciechowski, a former Duke player (1995-98) and now a Krzyzewski assistant. "Everything. That's what makes him the best, because people can't do that.

"It's contagious. How can you not play hard or be passionate when a Hall of Fame coach—a coach in his mid-fifties with a family, three daughters, and a grandson—is on the floor pounding it? You have to be lifeless not to want it that way."

THE GAME OF BASKETBALL

Why do you play a game? I play a game to see how good we can be.

DEFENSE

A sign prominent in the Duke locker room during the 1987–88 season provided what endures as a touchstone sentiment for the program: NO ONE PENETRATES OUR DEFENSE. Krzyzewski employs a man-to-man defensive scheme predicated on a ball-you-man approach. Constant help for teammates is provided. Talking to one another about positions and movements on the court is central to the common effort.

The Blue Devils are outstanding at denying the passing lanes. Their ball pressure further disrupts opposing offenses, making it difficult to feed the post, and forcing turnovers that fuel Duke's fastbreak.

"Against a lot of systems you can pass the ball around and some player on the floor won't guard the ball as well as the others," Dave Bliss said after losing to Duke while coaching at Southern Methodist. "It gives you a rest, an oasis. But there's no oasis against Duke. There's no place to put the ball where you know it's safe."

March 1988, on defense as Duke plays it, Rick Bonnell, *Charlotte Observer*:

You move as the ball moves, and when everyone is moving together like that, it's really a beautiful thing to watch.

March 1992, prior to the East Regional semifinal against Seton Hall, after saying a team being "emotionally ready" is the single most important quality to have:

Certainly, defense is the thing that wins for you. That's how we get our emotion.

PERSONAL FOULS

Duke thrives on getting to the foul line on offense, often attacking the basket with dribble penetration. The Blue Devils place equal stress on keeping opponents off the line. Krzyzewski considers the latter a "critical" aspect of playing intelligent basketball. His teams practice situations in which they have six fouls and must strive to play tough defense without incurring a seventh that would put the opposition on the line with a one-and-one opportunity.

Six Krzyzewski squads, including the last two, were so good at achieving this balance they made more free throws on the season than opponents even attempted. All told, only eighteen other ACC teams managed such a positive ratio of foul line–offense to foul shots allowed, since Krzyzewski entered the league in 1980–81.

Christian Laettner's performance against Kentucky in the 1992 NCAA East Regional final—10 for 10 from both floor and line, including the winning shot—capped one of the greatest games ever played.

January 1988:

The worst thing we can do is put the (other) team in a one-and-one.

January 1988, dismissing the notion that a team has fouls to waste:

I've never understood that, when commentators talk about that. One-and-ones are a major concern, because you can't play any defense if the other team is on the foul line.

FLOOR SLAP

Slapping the floor with both hands to signify a key defensive stand is, like the knocking of closed fists between players and coach during pre-game introductions, a characteristic non-verbal message in Duke basketball. Krzyzewski's earlier teams were more apt to employ the floor slap, though current point guard Jason Williams seems disposed toward the gesture.

March 1988, after defeating North Carolina, 65-61, in the ACC Tournament title game. With a 4-point lead and his team tiring, Krzyzewski pointed both index fingers toward the ground, and all five Duke players responded by slapping the floor at the Greensboro Coliseum:

When they were doing it earlier in the year, they didn't mean it, so I told them to quit. They would do it and just play our regular defense. But when you slap the floor like that, it should mean this is a key exchange and you put everything on the line.

OFFENSE

Duke's offense hasn't always operated as proficiently as its defense. In fact, it's when the defense is thriving, creating turnovers and hurried shots, that the Blue Devil attack is most effective.

Still, Duke led the ACC in free throw accuracy four times, field goal accuracy five times, and scoring nine times in Krzyzewski's first twenty seasons. The Devils paced the conference in scoring offense each year from 1997 through 2000, their 91.8 point average in 1999 was best in the ACC in a quarter century. The 1999 squad's 24.7 point victory margin was largest in conference history.

November 1986, Keith Drum, *Durham Morning Herald*:

Our offense is based on thinking. If you can really think on the court, then you have as much freedom as your abilities will allow. What you try to do is create roles for

Johnny Dawkins, the second-leading scorer in ACC history, here almost guarded by Georgia Tech's Mark Price.

your players. Not numbered roles or titled positions, but you try to say, "Look, here is where you're successful, now in this frame of reference you can do whatever the defense allows you, so read the defense."

THREE-POINT SHOT

Krzyzewski was an early critic of the 3-pointer, instituted in 1986–1987. He was less opposed to the shot itself than to the abrupt manner in which it was added, and the questionable wisdom of altering the game at the height of its popularity. Certainly, Duke teams quickly embraced the 3-pointer as an integral part of the action, extending their defense to contest the shot, and employing it heavily themselves. The Blue Devils made at least 36.5 percent of their threes every year since the shot was introduced, and paced the ACC in accuracy and attempts each season from 1998 through 2000.

January 1983, on an experimental 3-pointer employed by the ACC:
You should reward people for doing a difficult thing. You'd probably reward a window-washer more if he was on the twentieth floor than the first floor.

Early in his career at Duke, Krzyzewski had minimal talent and a seemingly inflexible approach.

April 1986, on institution of the 3-pointer:

I'm shocked that something like this has been passed at this time. To me, the game seems to be great right now. This is a revolutionary change and I don't think it's good for the game right now. We've just had a year of no chaos, and now we're introducing chaos. There are a lot of major coaches shocked by this. It could have more impact on the game than the shot clock. I'm not for it, and I'm really against the timing of the decision.

Summer 1988, on the newly installed 3-point shots acting "like magic" to produce "momentum streaks":

They hit, you hit, then everybody's going crazy.

INSIDE THE GAME

January 1985:

I have a plan of action, but the game is a game of adjustments.

March 1987:

I don't think we surprise people. We try to out-execute them.

January 1987:

When you're running up and down the court you're not thinking as much.

March 2000:

We got to the line a lot. Now, how did we get to the line? Did we have Duke officials? That's the way some people see it. Or did we actually do some things in the game to bring that about, like drive more?

January 1988:

Somewhere in the Virginia game we started to lose some of the zip in our game. It's a nice Polish word to use—some of our zipski.

SIDELINED

First alerted by leg and foot problems, Krzyzewski underwent surgery on October 21, 1994 to repair a ruptured disk in his

back. By then, preseason practice had begun for a team replacing two starters, including Grant Hill, from a group that reached the 1994 NCAA title game. Told a normal recovery period was six to twelve weeks, the coach returned to work within two. He wore a back brace and moved stiffly. By early December he vowed not to discuss the matter further, lest he foster "an atmosphere of excuse."

Following back, ankle and hip surgeries, Krzyzewski is almost as active on the bench in his younger days, pictured here.

But by January Krzyzewski lost twenty pounds and was exhausted. Prodded by his wife, doctors, and Tom Butters, Duke's athletic director, following a 75–70 home loss to Clemson on January 4, he decided to sit out the remainder of the season. Duke, 9–3 at the time, lost 15 of its last 19 games and sank from first to last in the span of a year. Near season's end Krzyzewski conducted a heavily attended, locally televised press conference to announce he was well and determined to learn from his near-burnout. Later the school successfully petitioned the NCAA to attribute the final 19 games to interim coach Pete Gaudet. The Devils' 18 losses that season were a school record.

October 1994, on back pain that led to surgery:

What it is, is basically a pain in the butt. Literally and figuratively. I may have been that to other people. I'm being punished.

March 1995, at his press conference:

I was very scared . . . I had never in my life not

been able to just go after something. I was so exhausted that I didn't have any energy. And I couldn't believe it was just my back. Polacks have strong backs.

TEAMS

September 1999:
The 1992 team was a great basketball team. I would put them up against anybody.

January 26, 1991, on 1975 and 1976 squads that combined for a 63–1 record at Indiana, where he'd been a graduate assistant in 1975:

Indiana, when they made a mistake, you were astounded. (Quinn) Buckner out there, I thought was as good a leader as you could have. I'm not sure anybody, any team, was as good over a two-year period as that team. It was like a science.

Duke's 1992 title made it the only repeat NCAA champion since UCLA in the early 1970s.

The thing you have to marvel about with that team is what they did in the Big Ten.

September 1999, on the 1999 squad that finished 37–2 and reached the NCAA title game:

I know we were really good last year. We weren't great. You need to establish more than one or two records. You have to be good for more than one season. I don't know if that happens anymore.

ATLANTIC COAST CONFERENCE

The ACC was founded in 1953 by eight schools that withdrew from the sprawling, seventeen-member Southern Conference, the first league to hold its own postseason tournament. Half the original members, the so-called "Big Four," are located in North Carolina—Duke, UNC-Chapel Hill, North Carolina State, and Wake Forest. Over the years North Carolina and Duke led the way as the ACC emerged as the nation's perennially toughest league. ACC teams have reached the NCAA Final Four thirty-two times, including Duke in 1999 and UNC in 2000, and won seven titles. No other conference has had as many Final Four entrants overall, or sent squads as often in the modern era—twenty times since 1981. Two or more ACC teams reached the NCAA Tournament's Sweet 16 each year since 1980, an unmatched run. Since 1991 every ACC member made at least one NCAA appearance, testament to top-to-bottom balance and competitiveness. Today there are nine ACC members—the North Carolina schools plus Clemson, Florida State, Georgia Tech, Maryland, and Virginia.

September 1999:
As much as I love Duke, I love the ACC.

September 1999, on a perceived insult to the ACC by getting only three teams in the 1999 NCAA Tournament:
There are not thirty teams better out there, at large, however many they come up with. Because the league chews you up, tears you up.

September 1999, on NCAA tournament invitations:
You can't let numbers do the talking. I don't care what kind of formulas you put up, the reality is, you go 8-8 in the ACC, you should go. Case closed.

Students at Cameron crowd so close to courtside their body paint and perspiration sometimes shower reporters on press row.

January 1997, after a win at North Carolina State's 1949-vintage Reynolds Coliseum, replaced in November 1999 by a new off-campus arena:
I've always been really impressed with the State fans. What a league and what an environment! We get that kind of support, too. I admire it.

March 1988:
The top four in the Big Ten, the top three in the Big East, the first division in the ACC—then you're a national title contender.

Summer 1988:
I love the ACC. Again, I'm not saying it's always the best conference ability-wise, but it's always one of the best. There's a class about the ACC. You feel a part of something that's beyond your school.

March 1988, on the eve of the ACC Tournament in Greensboro, where the event takes over the town:
It's just ACC basketball. I never knew anything like that before I came here.

February 1992:
Our league is good, and it's always been good. It proves itself at the end of each year.

OFFICIALS

The volatility of Krzyzewski's emotions is most evident in his relations with game officials. He's not averse to criticizing referees from the opening play of a game, even an exhibition contest. Up 25 points, he'll still gripe about calls. Sometimes he'll spend a good portion of a timeout standing outside the team huddle talking to or more likely yelling or glaring at an official. He's apt to focus on the least experienced member of a three-man crew and, like a wolf culling a victim from a herd, challenge him regularly in hopes of gaining a break.

Following a 1984 game against North Carolina in which Dean Smith appeared to have great latitude in leaving the coaching area, the young Duke coach decried a "double standard" in ACC officiating. The incident proved something of a turning point in modern ACC history; afterward Krzyzewski's program was freer to pursue its physical, hands-on defensive style.

There have been times, as during a home victory over Arizona in 1990, when Krzyzewski grew so incensed with an official he had to be physically restrained by others, though such incidents are rare lately. The technical fouls, once plentiful, have grown few and far between as well.

Understanding nuances of rules and interpretation are vital strategic concerns for Krzyzewski, here discussing a point with longtime official Lenny Wirtz.

January 1984, after a 79-73 home loss in which Krzyzewski got a technical at game's end while Smith got none despite twice leaving the bench area to pound on the scorer's table, the second time hitting a button that caused the game score to jump by 20 points on the overhead scoreboard:

There was not a person on our bench who was pointing at officials or banging on the scorer's table or having everybody running around on their bench. So let's get some things straight around here and quit the double standard that sometimes exists in this league. All right?

January 1996 to official Bob Donato:

Hey Bob! Make your call or don't! Be decisive!

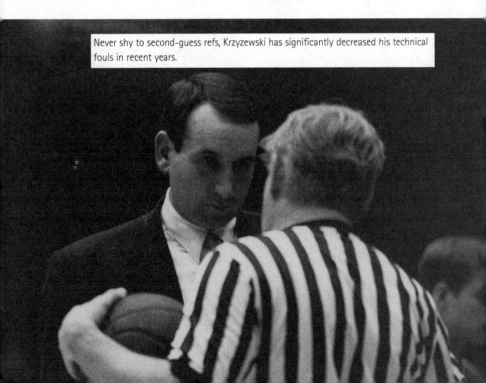

Never shy to second-guess refs, Krzyzewski has significantly decreased his technical fouls in recent years.

February 1989, following an 81–76 loss at Georgia Tech:

I really thought it was a well-officiated game. The officials don't hit free throws for you.

January 1996, to officials as Duke left the court following a 51-48 loss at Clemson in which a late traveling call on wing Ricky Price proved crucial:

You killed us! You killed us!

January 1990, to officials during a 96-91 win at Georgia Tech:

It's a goddamn homer call!

January 1989 after a win over last-place Maryland in which he got a technical foul for protesting a no-call:

It was a stupid, stupid technical on my part. I should be spanked for that one.

February 11, 1985, on officials' busy schedules:

We talk about having teams fresh at the end of the year. I can't believe some of these guys, with their schedules, can remain fresh.

March 1999, Elizabeth Oliver, *Fifty Plus*:

I believe there's someone bigger than me. I believe in God. I believe that everyone is a human being, except maybe officials, though they're human, too, once they take off their striped shirts.

SECOND
SEASON

I think you stress having fun and playing together, and attacking. Not playing conservative. You can't be afraid to lose in the NCAAs.

THE ACC TOURNAMENT

The ACC Tournament was once derided as a meaningless spectacle that detracted from regular season play and weakened teams entering the NCAA Tournament. But by the mid-1960s it was a competitive and financial success. Today, virtually every major conference has a postseason tournament. Duke won eleven ACC Tournament titles in the league's first forty-seven years, five under Krzyzewski—1986, 1988, 1992, 1999, and 2000. The Blue Devils have a .641 winning percentage (25–14) in the neutral-court event during Krzyzewski's twenty-year tenure.

March 1991:

Coming down here, the first couple of years I was just amazed at how it took over the region. I've fallen in love with it. I'm very proud to be associated with it.

Christian Laettner was Duke's pivotal player when the Blue Devils won consecutive NCAA titles.

NCAA TOURNAMENT

Duke appeared in the NCAA Tournament sixteen times in Mike Krzyzewski's first twenty years as head coach. After missing his first three years, the Blue Devils were in sixteen of the next seventeen NCAAs, including eleven in a row from 1984 through 1994. Krzyzewski's fifty tournament wins are tops among active coaches and second all-time to Dean Smith's sixty-five in thirty-six years. His .781 NCAA winning percentage (50–14) leads active coaches.

The Blue Devils routinely lessen the physical demands of practice as the regular season ends so players' bodies and minds are fresher entering tournament play. Krzyzewski counsels players to limit contact during the NCAAs with all but immediate family; to approach each weekend of play as a discrete tournament in itself; to respect each opponent; to play to win; to take nothing for granted; and to focus inwardly. "Definitely, your primary focus is on Duke," he says.

March 1997:

There's an innocence that's captured in this tournament that's remarkable, and really the essence of sports.

March 2000, on the tournament selection committee and its judgment in choosing the field and assigning seeds:

Not all of them are basketball people. They may

like basketball, and they have the highest level of integrity and high SATs and all that, but they're not all basketball people. And they don't have their finger on the pulse of the game. I think in order to make this tournament the very best, we should always have people governing it and choosing the teams for this tournament who have their finger on the pulse of the game.

February 1994:
I think you stress having fun and playing together, and attacking. Not playing conservative. You can't be afraid to lose in the NCAAs.

March 1991, recalling the electric attire worn by the head coach of unheralded Mississippi Valley State, which nearly upset top-ranked Duke in the opening round of the '86 NCAAs:
I dream of Lafayette Stribling walking in his blue shoes.

March 1999:
People believe in miracles in March.

March 1991, after North Carolina's Dean Smith implied Duke had an easy path to the Final Four, which both teams ultimately reached by month's end:
I think coaches shouldn't talk about other people's seeds. Talk about your own.

August 1991, on Smith's comments:

Maybe the best thing for us is to just trade places after everybody's picked . . . Our road to the championship game was certainly as difficult, if not more difficult, than any other ACC team. You may look at other teams and say their path was the easiest. Who cares?

FINAL FOUR

Duke went to the Final Four three times under head coach Vic Bubas (1963, 1964, and 1966) and once under Bill Foster (1978). During Krzyzewski's first twenty years the Blue Devils made eight appearances—1986, 1988, 1989, 1990, 1991, 1992, 1994, 1999.

Only North Carolina (15), UCLA (14), and Kentucky (13) achieved more Final Four visits than Duke's dozen. Only UCLA under John Wooden had more consecutive Final Four appearances (nine from 1967–75) than Krzyzewski's five in the late 1980s and early 1990s. Only Wooden (12) and North Carolina's Dean Smith (11) have taken more teams to the Final Four, and both are retired.

March 1986:

It combines the best basketball of the whole country. It's the only time when high school coaches, junior college coaches, and small college coaches are all in the same place. It means all parts of the game. A lot of coaches better than me have never made it there.

March 1991, on ignoring his 0–4 record in the Final Four to that point:
I think if I start thinking about stuff like that, I may start coaching like there's more pressure on me. . . . For me, I try to stay the same. I'm intense all year long.

March 1994:
It's not like we've won every Final Four we've been in, so it's not like we have the recipe or anything.

NEVADA–LAS VEGAS

Jerry "Tark the Shark" Tarkanian and his Nevada-Las Vegas program reached the height of their prowess at the dawn of the 1990s. The talented and mature Runnin' Rebels of Larry Johnson, Stacey Augmon, Anderson Hunt, and Greg Anthony smothered opponents defensively and attacked them relentlessly on offense.

A relatively inexperienced Duke squad met UNLV for the 1990 NCAA title and lost 103–73, still the most decisive defeat in championship game history. Freshman point guard Bobby Hurley, ill prior to the contest, said he dreamt of sharks afterward.

The following season UNLV was undefeated and top-ranked in the polls, and virtually conceded the championship before the NCAAs began. But Duke won, 79–77, when the teams met again in the 1991 Final Four. Christian Laettner had 28 points, 20 in the first half, and the decisive free throws with 12.7 seconds left. Hurley hit a key 3-pointer, down 76–71 with 2:16 remaining. Unsung senior Greg Koubek fronted Johnson, the choice of many as national player of the year, and helped hold him to 13 points, 10 below his average. The Blue Devils followed their stunning upset of the defending champions by beating Kansas for the NCAA title two days later.

April 1990, following a 30-point trouncing in the national title game:

They were just totally in control. I think it's the

best that a team has ever played against me as a coach. I'm in awe of what they did tonight. I don't know if you really realize how good they were defensively. They were great.

Tonight was not a game of X's and O's, it was a game of complete focus. There was really not much we could do tonight. They would not let us do anything.

October 1990, on the lingering effects of the blowout by UNLV the previous spring:

There's this twitch I have.

March 1991, asked how much time he'd like to prepare to face UNLV, on a 45-game winning streak:

I'd like three years.

March 1991, on the theme of CBS' coverage:

That's their show—Who can beat Vegas? It's like a mini-series.

March 1991, following a 79–77 victory over UNLV in the Final Four:

I'm not sure we could beat them again. But, like last year, we only play once.

CHAMPIONSHIPS

The Blue Devils reached the NCAA title game six times—in 1986, 1990, 1991, 1992, 1994, and 1999. They lost to Louisville in 1986, to UNLV in 1990 by the largest margin in championship game history, to Arkansas in 1994, and to UConn in 1999. They won the national championship in 1991, beating Kansas, 72–65, and again in 1992, defeating Michigan, 71–51.

No other program since UCLA, which won seven straight from 1967 through 1973, has captured consecutive NCAA titles. And only three coaches won more championships than Krzyzewski—UCLA's John Wooden (10), Kentucky's Adolph Rupp (4), and Indiana's Bob Knight (3).

Krzyzewski's teams also have reached the championship game in the ACC Tournament nine times, winning in 1986, 1988, 1992, 1999, and 2000.

Krzyzewski has taken eight of twenty Duke teams to the Final Four, including five in a row from 1988-92.

March 1989:

That's not the thing I want more than anything else. I'd have to have my head examined to think that's the one thing I want more than anything else, a national championship. I start getting philosophical. I want good family, good health. I want consistent performance and I want the truth, much more than I want a national championship.

1989, on Duke failing in the Final Four for the third time in four years, running the school's record to seven trips without a title:

Blame me. I'm the constant around here. I've been around when we couldn't win the big one.

October 1991, asked if his daily life has changed since winning the national championship, such as getting more attention at the supermarket:

They're charging me more.

April 1992, to fans gathered at Cameron Indoor Stadium to celebrate a 71–51 victory over Michigan in the national championship game:

Last year, I said I wonder where we'll put the second banner. We've got to find out, don't we? I'm probably stupid for saying this, but I wonder where a third one might go.

November 1992, recalling Bobby Hurley's broken foot and a foot injury to Grant Hill that slowed but never derailed the 34–2 team of 1992:

The injuries kind of provided the adversity. I thought that was good.

Grant Hill (1991-94) was a key performer on three teams that reached the NCAA title game, but didn't fully appreciate his own talent until reaching the NBA.

July 1996:

The best teams are teams in any sport that lose themselves in the team. The individuals lose their identity. And their identities come about as a result of being in the team first.

Trajan Langdon carried Duke in the '99 title game against Connecticut, but committed a decisive turnover in the waning seconds. Krzyzewski adamantly defended calling the play.

I'll give you an example . . . I'd like to average 18 points a game. I feel that if I average 18 points a game, my team's going to be better. And that's the way a lot of people think. If so-and-so gets 18, they're going to be better.

I think you have to look at it just the opposite. Like I want to win the game, and by me being a potential 18-point scorer, by throwing myself into winning the game, I'm going to score 18 points.

I don't know if that's crazy or not, but that's what Laettner did. That's what Dawkins did. By winning, by trying to win, they scored their 18.

That is being a champion, I think. To actually believe that and go about it.

March 1993, entering the NCAA Tournament as the two-time defending champions:

Certainly a story that's waiting to be told is when a champion falls in any sport. We have to look at it as if it's nothing personal. People are waiting to close a chapter. We have to use that to our advantage—we don't want anyone to close any darn chapters on us.

In other words, they're almost waiting for you to lose. There's people out there, a lot of people, waiting for someone new to win. We have to make sure we're not those people.

March 1993, on a squad that led wire to wire, enduring injuries to become the first repeat NCAA champions since UCLA two decades earlier:

Last year's team was very unusual. Last year's team was one of the best teams to come out of this conference.

June 1999, on a decisive last play in a loss to Connecticut in the NCAA title game:

We felt we put our best at that point and they met our best. I'm fine with that.

PEOPLE IN THE GAME

You can't teach talent, but you can help mold character. If you help mold a good character then that person is going to make good use of that talent. But you can't be molding character with 12, 13 guys. You have to have guys who are bringing these qualities in with them.

FANS

March 1999, returning from a loss to Connecticut in the 1999 NCAA title game to address fans gathered at mid-afternoon at Cameron:

We shared so much with you this year. That's what this place is all about—Cameron. I'm kind of a little bit choked up really. Because to have you now come here, to see so many of your faces. You're making a lot of noise and whatever, but more than that we can look at your faces and know that you're sharing with us. And I want to thank you for that. It really adds substance to what we do. It's really one of the reasons I love coaching here so much, because it's been that way at least for the nineteen years I've been here.

January 1994, after trying to stop a chant of "Over-rated!" directed at Maryland's Joe Smith, the eventual ACC rookie of the year, when he was at the foul line in a game Duke went on to win, 63–44:

There's 8 minutes and 23 seconds to go. You know what? It's just an indication to me, our team is 15–1 and nobody at Duke knows it. Where's the celebration for Chris Collins and Jeff Capel? Don't be yelling "over-rated" against any other team with 8:23 left. They could kick our butts. I'm a little bit disturbed about that. I don't think these kids have gotten the recognition they deserve.

March 1998, on seeing more Duke paraphernalia away from home than nearby, where North Carolina fans predominate:

The popularity of our program is great, not necessarily in our area.

August 1991, saying "Nothing surprises me" about fan reactions:

They go overboard. That's the bad stuff of it.

PEOPLE

TOMMY AMAKER

Harold "Tommy" Amaker, from Falls Church, Virgina, joined Duke in 1982–83 and started immediately at point guard. By Amaker's junior year the Blue Devils reached the NCAA title game. Amaker, slender at six feet and 155 pounds, was remarkably steady with the ball, averaging 2.1 assists for every turnover. He paced Duke in steals each season he played and had 259 in his career, most in modern school history. Voted the 1987 national defensive player of the year, Amaker was a calm leader and an extension of Krzyzewski's will on the court. Currently, after serving as a Duke assistant coach for nine years, Amaker is head coach at Seton Hall.

Tommy Amaker was the starting point guard and floor leader when Krzyzewski's program first broke onto the national scene.

June 1999:

Tommy started ahead of almost everyone in our program ever in his maturity level.

April 1993, six years after Amaker graduated:

Tommy Amaker is the best kid who's ever played for me.

January 1987. While recruiting Johnny Dawkins, Krzyzewski noticed a point guard from W. T. Woodson High, John Feinstein, *Washington Post*:

He was tiny, I mean really small. But he understood the game so well, I was amazed. He had just finished his sophomore year in high school, but you could see it. When the game was over I was introduced to his mother. I said: "Mrs. Amaker, your son is going to look great in Duke blue."

October 1987, on Amaker telling him to shut up:

I never tried that when I played for Knight.

WILLIAM AVERY

William Avery was a 6–2, 180-pound guard from Augusta, Georgia. Academic deficiencies caused Avery to attend prep school before enrolling at Duke. He was primarily a backup in 1998, then started every game at point in 1999 as the Blue Devils went 37–2 and reached the NCAA title game.
Quick, strong, and a fearless shooter, Avery averaged nearly two assists for every turnover as a sophomore, while contributing

Articulate, talented, and polished, forward Shane Battier "is what Duke's all about," said teammate Chris Carrawell.

14.9 points per game. He left school with two years of eligibility remaining, and was taken by Minnesota in the first round of the NBA draft. He's still in the NBA.

June 1999, after Avery decided to turn pro despite Krzyzewski's publicly stated advice to the contrary:

I love William. I loved who he was becoming, both on and off the court. I hate to see that process stop, and as a teacher and coach I feel badly about that. That's how my feelings were hurt, not in some other way.

June 1997, mentioning that Avery was an honor student in grade school:

He's one of those kids I wish college administrators would try to understand more.

SHANE BATTIER

Shane Battier, a 6–8, 225-pound forward, was considered by many the nation's top prep talent when he joined Duke in 1997–98. Versatile, polished, and a keen defender, the Michigan native started almost every game of his career. Twice chosen the best defender in college ball, the articulate Battier "really blossomed" as a junior, according to Krzyzewski. In 2000 Battier, admired even by opposing coaches for his vocal on-court leadership, became an all-around offensive threat, pacing Duke in scoring (17.4). He also heads a student-athlete group seeking a greater voice in NCAA governance.

March 2000:

I truly admire some of the qualities of my players, not just their jumping ability or whatever. I know I wasn't as good as Shane Battier when I was in college, or as mature. Are you kidding me?

June 1998:

To me he had as great an impact as any freshman in the league. We were 15-1. This kid was the backbone of our defense. He didn't score a lot, but he didn't have to score a lot.

June 1997:

Shane is a throwback to understanding the complete game and getting satisfaction from doing all the little things that will produce a win.

ELTON BRAND

Elton Brand played at Duke in 1998 and 1999. At 6-8 and 245 pounds he was among the fastest Blue Devils, with large hands, a deft shooting touch, a calm demeanor, and sufficient toughness and strength to hold his own in the post. A broken foot cut short Brand's freshman year, causing him to miss 15 mid-season games. As a sophomore the genial Brand led the ACC in field goal percentage (.620) and was second in scoring (17.7) and rebounding (9.8). The 1999 ACC and national player of the year, Brand was the first Duke player ever to leave early for the pros. Chicago made him the first pick in the NBA draft, unmatched at Duke since Art Heyman in 1963.

June 1999, on Brand leaving early:

Elton felt somewhat guilty, I really believe that. Elton and his mom, they wanted to make sure they weren't offending people at Duke. I thought Elton and his mom were amazingly sensitive to the whole situation. But it was obvious what they wanted to do.

June 1999, just days before the NBA draft:

I think Elton has an unbelievable upside. People who characterize him as just a power player are so wrong.

CHRIS BURGESS

Chris Burgess came to Duke with Avery, Battier, and Brand, touted by some as the best of the lot. The 6-10 Californian never established himself in the starting lineup in two years at Duke. Burgess transferred to Utah following the 1999 season, accompanied by his father's denunciation of Krzyzewski for duplicity.

Billed as the nation's top freshman class in 1997-98: Elton Brand (left), Chris Burgess (top), William Avery (bottom, center), and Shane Battier.

June 1997, prior to Burgess' freshman season:

I think he's really as good coming in as Danny (Ferry) or Christian (Laettner). But those guys didn't have the amazing pressure that Chris Burgess has had to carry for a year. I've seen him be a tremendous competitor. I've also seen him play like he doesn't care.

CHRIS CARRAWELL

Chris Carrawell, a versatile 6–6 wing, served as a complementary player from 1997 through 1999. During high school in St. Louis and later at Duke, he suffered from repeated shoulder injuries. Finally healthy and central to the team's plans, in 2000, Carrawell led surprising Duke to a No.1 ranking and was named ACC player of the year.

March 2000:

I love that kid. He's my friend for life.

January 2000, following a 30-point effort in an overtime victory over North Carolina State:

Carrawell is a magnificent warrior. I'm truly honored to be his coach. He's really developed into such a tough kid.

VINCE CARTER

Vince Carter played at North Carolina from 1996–98, and was an all-ACC player as a junior, after which he turned pro. Carter has since gone on to stardom with the NBA's Toronto Raptors.

Vince Carter hung around Chapel Hill for three years, then became a star in the NBA.

March 1997:

Other than the point guard, I'd really take Carter to lock up anybody . . . Potentially he's a great, great defensive player.

CHRIS COLLINS

Chris Collins, a 6–3 guard, played at Duke from 1993 through 1996. Cocky but a bit slow afoot, the son of former NBA star and coach Doug Collins, Chris was a fearless shooter and fiery competitor. His best year came as a senior, when he averaged 16.3 points in Krzyzewski's comeback season. Collins currently is an assistant coach at Duke.

January 1996, after Collins hit a long 3-pointer from in front of the Duke bench to win a game, 71–70, at N.C. State, the shot bouncing repeatedly on the rim before going in:

He almost stepped on my toe. And, really, he didn't do what he was supposed to do.

BOBBY CREMINS

Bobby Cremins was head coach at Georgia Tech from 1982 through 2000, after which he was forced out by an unsupportive athletic director and three losing records in four seasons. Cremins, boyishly likeable and open, built the Tech program from a doormat to a national power, culminating in 1990 with the sole Final Four appearance in school history. Cremins won three ACC titles, took ten teams to the NCAAs, was 354–237 at Tech, and produced players Mark Price, John Salley, Dennis Scott, Kenny Anderson, and Stephon Marbury, among others.

"God forbid we were chasing the same girl, we'd kill each other," admiring Georgia Tech coach Bobby Cremins said of his competitive relationship with Krzyzewski.

February 2000, after wearing a gold tie and blue sportcoat:

Bobby Cremins, I can remember being at his gym and my gym when games were 47 to 45 and we were absolutely awful. And he built his program into a national program. Some of the great games in the history of the ACC were Duke-Georgia Tech games in the 1980s and early 1990s. I respect that.

I love him. I really believe that whole situation

throughout the year was not handled right. Bobby Cremins deserves to go out like a champion, which he is.

JOHNNY DAWKINS

Johnny Dawkins was the first prominent recruit, and produced the first retired jersey number (24), of Krzyzewski's tenure. A high-waisted, 6–2 guard from Washington, D.C., Dawkins played from 1983 through 1986. Duke's career scoring leader with 2,556 points, he paced the Blue Devils in point production each year he played. His senior season the team reached the national title game and Dawkins won the Naismith Award as national player of the year. Following nine NBA seasons Dawkins returned to Durham, and is associate head coach under Krzyzewski.

March 1986, on the eve of the NCAA Tournament:
I feel about as close to Johnny Dawkins as any player who's played for me . . . His only weakness is he's not Polish.

March 1986:
I think he's been the catalyst. It's not saying anything against anybody else. It's just that Johnny has special qualities. He's such a good player right now, and he's done it within the team. He's brought other good players and a sense of confidence. Having Johnny on the team makes everybody better. His mere presence gives a little more confidence.

February 1986, prior to retiring Dawkin's jersey:
When we're back here walking with canes, we'll say, "Hey, that kid was one of the best." He's a fabulous player. I'm a better coach because of Johnny Dawkins, I'll tell you that.

VINNY DEL NEGRO

Vinny Del Negro was a little-noted, 6–5 guard who languished on North Carolina State's bench his first two seasons under Jim Valvano. Forced into the lineup in 1987 when other options failed, Del Negro became a star and was first team all-ACC as a senior in 1988. A second-round NBA draft choice by Sacramento, he remains in the NBA.

February 1988:

He's a hell of a player. He's cool. He's always in the game. He plays at a steady pace . . . Playing against kids like Del Negro, I like that. It's a privilege for me.

TIM DUNCAN

Tim Duncan, the ultimate recruiting "sleeper," arrived unheralded from St. Croix in the Virgin Islands and became a star at Wake Forest from 1994 through 1997. Wake won ACC titles his sophomore and junior years. Twice named ACC player of the year (1996 and 1997), the 6–10 Duncan was 1997 national player of the year. During his career the Demon Deacons won eight of nine against Duke.

Tim, I thought we did a decent job on him and he got 26 (points) and 14 (rebounds). Imagine what he would have gotten if we didn't play really hard.

DANNY FERRY

Danny Ferry arrived at Duke for the 1986 season with an impeccable basketball pedigree. His father, Bob, played and coached in the NBA, and at Maryland's DeMatha High Ferry was coached by highly respected Morgan Wootten. Versatile at 6–10, Ferry was among the first big men to take full advantage of the new 3-point shot. He scored an ACC-record 58 points at Miami in his senior season, when he was national player of the year. Ferry, whose jersey number 35 was retired by Duke, paced the Blue Devils in scoring and rebounding from 1987–89, and in assists in 1987. He led the Blue Devils to the Final Four in 1988 and 1989, seasons he was voted ACC player of the year. He currently plays in the NBA.

July 1988, prior to Ferry's senior season:
I think Danny's best asset is his mind.

January 1988:
He plays the game the way it was meant to be played. There's no confinement to his game. He can play outside and inside. . . . Most sons of coaches have that, but they're all 6–1, 6–2.

Danny Ferry carried Duke as a sophomore in 1987, a key season in sustaining Krzyzewski's program.

February 1988, John Feinstein, *Washington Post:*

Danny makes every big play for us. If we need a 3-point shot, he makes it. If we need a rebound, he gets it. If we need him to open things up with his passing, he does it. We knew he could be a special player when he got here if he worked hard. He's done the work and this is the result.

GRANT HILL

Grant Hill gradually emerged as a star at Duke from 1991–94. A stunning combination of skill, size (6–8), talent, and intelligence, Hill started virtually every game for which he was healthy. During his career the Blue Devils won two NCAA titles and reached another national championship game in 1994. In his senior season Hill finally asserted himself and was ACC player of the year and a consensus first team all-American. Duke retired his No. 33 jersey. Hill currently plays in the NBA, where he is a repeat all-pro.

Grant Hill, among the most gifted Duke players ever, deferred to others until becoming a senior in 1994.

February 1994, Hill's senior season:

The first time I saw Grant play in high school, I felt that he would be the most talented player I've ever recruited. He's a beautiful player. His potential is still not even close to being developed.

February 1994, after a win at Wake Forest:

Grant is almost too unselfish. He's trying to get everyone going.

March 1994:

He's the best defensive player we've ever had. He's the best defensive player I've ever seen in college. It's not even close.

June 1990:

His ego is such that he understands that scoring averages aren't that important, and the beauty of the game is putting it all together and winning it. He already understands that. I think he has a maturity level above that of a normal freshman. He's class all the way.

THOMAS HILL

Thomas Hill played alongside Bobby Hurley in the Duke backcourt from 1990–93. A strong outside shooter, the Texan took a back seat to teammates. His best season was '93, when he averaged 15.7 points, third on the squad.

November 1989 after a 102–66 win over Canisius:

He was spectacular in the simplicity of his game.

BOBBY HURLEY

Bobby Hurley, the son of Bob Hurley, a successful and highly demanding high school coach in New Jersey, started all but one game in which he appeared at Duke from 1990–93. Aggressive to the point of recklessness and diminutive at six feet and 165 pounds, Hurley nevertheless led his first three teams to the NCAA title game. Duke won in 1991 and 1992. He completed his career as the modern NCAA assist leader with 1,076, and as the unofficial modern ACC leader in turnovers with 534. A consensus first team all-American in 1993, Hurley had his number 11 jersey retired, and was taken by Sacramento in the first round of the NBA draft. His pro career was cut short when he was victimized in a severe auto accident, from which he recovered.

Playmaker Bobby Hurley, a four-year starter, made up with effort, daring, and smarts what he lacked in size and strength.

January 1991:

Geez, I get letters from people saying I should bench him. I thought he led us to the Final Four last year.

June 1990:

Bobby's strength is creativity.

November 1992:

I identify with Bobby because of his background,

too. It's similar to how I grew up and I see so many (similarities to) the things in his group, not only his parents but the whole family structure around him. Like this weekend, there were about fifty people here from Jersey City. Judges, lawyers, policemen, FBI, family, they just came down to see Bobby in an intrasquad scrimmage. It was like a pilgrimage. And it wasn't because they then were going to get some great things. They just love Bobby. That structure, I've been privy to that in my own life—aunts and uncles and extended family and all that.

November 1992:
There are two words that I use in describing Bobby. One is "winner." That's an overused word, but not in this case. And then "daring."

February 1992, following Hurley's return from injury, on the effect of his presence:
Last night, you could actually see our guys running faster down the court because they thought they might get to score.

April 1993:
Coaching Bobby, I learned to be more daring. He was never afraid to do things. He gave me his heart and soul every time he went out on the court.

MICHAEL JORDAN

Michael Jordan played at North Carolina from 1982 through 1984, a period in which the Tar Heels were 6–1 against Duke, dropping only an ACC Tournament contest in 1984. Jordan made the winning shot in the 1982 NCAA title game, was a consensus All-American as a sophomore and junior, and the 1984 ACC and national player of the year. Jordan left school a year early, was taken in the first round by the Chicago Bulls, and retired in 1998 generally recognized as the greatest player in basketball history.

1984:

He's a very talented, gifted player who's a smart player and who works hard at developing both his mental and physical capabilities. The package is there. And he wants to get better. That's a unique situation. I admire him. I want to beat him, but I admire him too.

August 1992, after working with Jordan as an assistant on the U.S. Olympic "Dream Team":

Everyone talks about his dunks, jumping, whatever, and you should. When he's playing defense, it's at the highest level I have ever seen.

Krzyzewski lists Dukies Grant Hill and Shane Battier and North Carolina's Michael Jordan as the best defenders he's seen during his Durham tenure.

January 1982, following a loss to North Carolina in Jordan's freshman season:

Jordan was unbelievable. He was

just good the whole ballgame, but for a two- or three-minute stretch he broke it away for them.

BILLY KING

Billy King was the first Krzyzewski player to develop a national reputation primarily on the basis of defense. King, a 6–6 wing from Virginia, played at Duke from 1985–88. A modest scorer and miserable foul shooter (.479), King never made all-conference but in 1988 was voted the country's top defender. He throttled prominent scorers like North Carolina's Jeff Lebo, Notre Dame's David Rivers, and Temple's Mark Macon, and was a strong, vocal leader in the Duke locker room and on the court. King presently is general manager of the NBA's Philadelphia 76ers.

November 1988:

I think he got notoriety for his one-on-one matchups. His main ability was to coordinate our defense. He was a great communicator. He talked the best on the court. In following our basketball team and sitting at court level, you could hear our guys talking a lot. The guy talking most of the time was usually Billy. Some people talk and don't say very much, but when Billy talked on the court he usually said something that was very pertinent to what was going on. His talk helped everybody else.

February 1988, following a 70–61 victory over Notre Dame in which King shut down Rivers on national TV, breaking the smaller, quicker guard's 31-game streak of double-figure scoring efforts:

Billy was magnificent. I thought his concentration was incredible. David Rivers has some moves. If you don't concentrate, he'll be at the foul line all day.

BOB KNIGHT

Bob Knight was head coach at Army from 1966–71, and coached Krzyzewski there before moving to Indiana. Knight, who played at Ohio State from 1958–60, is one of six men to play and coach in a Final Four. In twenty-nine seasons Knight's Indiana teams were 661–240 and appeared in twenty-eight NCAA tournaments and five Final Fours, winning national titles in 1976, 1981, and 1987. Krzyzewski worked for Knight as a grad assistant at Indiana in 1974–75. The two remained close friends for many years, and the highly volatile Knight was considered Krzyzewski's mentor. The two split four meetings in head-to-head competition. The first Duke win, in the 1992 Final Four, apparently opened a rift between the coaches that exists to this day. Knight was fired for "uncivil, defiant, and unacceptable" behavior in September 2000.

March 1980, on taking the Duke job:

I'm a young coach, and I've been influenced by a lot of coaches, Coach Knight most of all. But I'm not Bobby Knight. I'm a different person. I teach many of his principles, but we all use different techniques to get those ideas across.

Bob Knight, nicknamed "The General," and his most successful protege, nicknamed "Captain."

March 1991:

Coach and I are very close. But we're different personalities. He likes to hunt and I like to go to the beach. He likes to fish and I like to eat fish. My only pet peeve is when somebody asks if I called him to find out what I should do.

Late 1980s:

I get all these Knight-disciple questions. When am I going to be an apostle?

January 1981:

I called Knight at halftime. He was yelling at a kid at the time.

March 1987, discussing his "constant" contact with Knight:

He certainly doesn't call me the things he did when I played for him.

March 1987:

When you have worked under Coach Knight, you get some stigmas put on you, good and bad. One thing is everybody thinks you're very disciplined, the kind of discipline people think of as being restrictive. I don't think that's what discipline means.

CHRISTIAN LAETTNER

No Duke player generated more adverse reaction than Christian Laettner, arguably the greatest Blue Devil ever. "Christian plays at a very high level of intensity," Krzyzewski said in 1991. Laettner, a multi-faceted, 6–11 New Yorker, played at Duke from 1989–92. He set a school record for field goal accuracy his freshman year, making 72.3 percent. Duke reached the Final Four in each of his seasons, winning national titles the last two. Smart, polished, arrogant, and fiercely competitive, Laettner led Duke in scoring and rebounding his last two seasons. Against Connecticut in 1990 and Kentucky in 1992 he made game-winning shots in overtime to send the Devils to the Final Four. As a senior Laettner was national player of the year, had his jersey number 32 retired by Duke, and was taken by Minnesota in the first round of the NBA draft. He presently plays in the NBA.

June 1994:

He liked to catch the ball and survey the scene, and it's hurt him some in the pros. I've talked to him about it. He should, when he catches it, shoot it if he's open. That's his mentality of trying to be in control. "OK, I'm going to catch it. Now, I have the ball and I am in control." And that's a personality thing that impacts negatively on him as a basketball player.

Testy but superbly productive, Christian Laettner ranks among the top handful of players in ACC history.

March 1992:

That's something that he's worked hard to overcome, that because he's from the Nichols School and 6-11 and white that he shouldn't be tough. But he is. The only athletic people in the game don't have to be black, and the only smart people don't have to be white.

March 1990, a week before Laettner made his shot to beat Connecticut and two years before he broke Kentucky hearts:

Christian's a very confident player. He's made so many big shots.

November 1992:

Laettner pretty much came with a fire in his eyes and a passion every ballgame.

March 1989:

Christian's drug test always comes back positive. I'm not poking fun at drug testing, but Christian is on a natural high. Why can't other kids play like that?

TRAJAN LANGDON

Trajan Langdon, the first prominent Division I player from Alaska, played at Duke from 1995–99. He actually arrived as a walk-on, having signed a baseball contract with the San Diego

Padres. The 6–3 Anchorage product missed the 1996 season due to a knee injury. Quiet, steady, and a consummate team player, Langdon was among the premier shooters in Blue Devil history, and his .862 career accuracy from the foul line is second-best by an ACC player. Langdon's senior season the Devils returned to the Final Four following a five-year absence. A three-time selection for first team all-ACC, Langdon was a first round draft pick by Cleveland in 1999 and is currently in the NBA.

Trajan Langdon, a self-made player from Alaska, finished as Duke's most prolific 3-point shooter and the ACC's second-best career free throw shooter.

June 1999, on the 1999 title game, decided after a key Langdon turnover on a much second-guessed play:

To me, in my time on the bench, it was obvious Langdon, we were riding Langdon. I don't care what we'd done the whole year, and (Elton) Brand being player of the year and whatever. There's no way we have a chance of winning that ballgame without Trajan Langdon. We're going to lose by 10, 12 points.

March 1999, with Steve Wojciechowski:

Absolutely I feel a special bond to Trajan Langdon . . . Wojo and Trajan over the last five years, they were the bridge to get us back playing at an elite state. I'll forever be indebted to them.

February 1997, after Langdon had 34 points in a home win over Clemson:
You can't be blind. That kid had one of the great nights in the history of the league. He was magnificent. . . . I'm proud of my team, but you have to go bonkers over what Trajan did.

DANNY MEAGHER

Dan Meagher, a 6–7 Canadian, was the only player from Krzyzewski's first full Duke recruiting class to become a long-term contributor. Meagher played forward from 1982–85. He never led a Blue Devil squad in any major statistical category, but set a scrappy, competitive tone that carried the program from consecutive losing seasons to consecutive NCAA appearances during his career.

December 1992:

Meagher was the toughest kid who ever played here.

January 1982, following a 99–61 thrashing at Louisville:

He wasn't intimidated. You get 14 rebounds against those guys, you're giving second and third effort. He took two great charges. You stand in and take a charge from Rodney McCray like he did, that takes guts. He showed excellent toughness, which is something we've not seen much of.

CHEROKEE PARKS

Cherokee Parks came from California dubbed the heir apparent to Christian Laettner as Duke's multi-purpose big man, but didn't match his predecessor's single-mindedness. The 6–11 Parks was a fine player from 1992–95, but also enjoyed being a college student. He did pace Duke squads once each in scoring, field goal accuracy, and free throw percentage, and three times in rebounding. Parks made second team all-ACC his last two years. Taken in the first round by Dallas in 1995, he remains in the NBA.

November 1991, after a Duke exhibition win over a team from the Soviet Union:

Cherokee is a peace activist. If there was a campus crusade for peace, Cherokee would be right there.

DEAN SMITH

Dean Smith won his first national championship in 1982, his seventh visit to the Final Four as head coach at North Carolina. Smith went to eleven Final Fours in all before retiring in 1997, and won a second NCAA title in 1993. Smith's Tar Heels won 879 games in thirty-six seasons, and were 24–14 against Krzyzewski's squads. Publicly Smith and Krzyzewski spoke admiringly of one another's programs, but there was a constant undercurrent of competitiveness, if not more, that often colored their comments.

June 1990, on North Carolina's 21,572-seat Dean E. Smith Student Activities Center:

What he's done is amazing, and that's why he's in

Dean Smith was an intense and sometimes maddening competitor whose program set the ACC standard for two decades.

the Hall of Fame and that's why it's not called Jones Center, it's called Smith Center. I mean, he had to do something pretty good for that to happen, and he did something that is great and he's been consistently excellent. He's a hell of a coach.

July 1996, on both coaches' losing records in the Final Four:
If he and I have choked, everyone should want to choke.

March 1988, on comparisons between the programs at Duke and the University of North Carolina:
You never beat him. You beat their team. I think I can hold my own one-on-one, but not against (Michael) Jordan and (Sam) Perkins and those guys.

February 1989:
I think I can beat him one-on-one. I think I'm in better shape. I'd post him inside.

March 1996. Smith denounced Duke students for chanting, with some justification, that Tar Heel Jeff McInnis was an "asshole" after the guard was ejected from a game at Cameron. The North Carolina coach also chided Duke administrators for not insisting on better student comportment:
I thought that his comments were to create an edge in other areas, because they were certainly

comments that came out of nowhere. There must be a hidden meaning.

QUIN SNYDER

Quin Snyder came to Duke from Mercer Island, Washington. His freshman year, 1986, the program reached its first Final Four. Snyder was a bit out of character as a playmaker, but even while struggling with his role helped Duke to Final Fours in 1988 and 1989, seasons in which he led the team in assists and steals. Throughout his career the 6-2 guard was troubled by crushing headaches and a combustible relationship with his coach. He ultimately returned to Duke and served as Krzyzewski's chief assistant until hired in 1999-2000 as head coach at Missouri.

Flanked by two former guards turned assistant coach—Quin Snyder (left), now head coach at Missouri, and Johnny Dawkins.

November 1987, following a Snyder dunk against an Italian national team in a 98-79 exhibition win:

I think someone pinched him in the butt when he made that dunk. I can't believe that.

March 1989:

There's not a kid who played here at Duke who has given me any more as a kid and player as Quin. Now, there's been a player (like) Johnny (Dawkins) who's had more to give, or Mark (Alarie). Quin gives me everything.

JIM VALVANO

Jim Valvano and Krzyzewski took parallel personal and career paths in paradoxically different directions. Both were from big-city ethnic families, Valvano an Italian from New York. Both played point guard in college near New York for successful coaches, Valvano at Rutgers for Bill Foster. Both proved themselves as mid-major head coaches near New York, Valvano at Iona. Both arrived at Triangle-area ACC schools in the spring of 1980, Valvano at North Carolina State. Both won NCAA titles after huge upsets, Valvano beating Houston in 1983. But Valvano reveled in celebrity and opportunity, while Krzyzewski clung to home, sport, and a sense of morality. The relationship changed when Valvano was stricken with fatal bone cancer, and the two became fast friends until he died in 1993 at age 46.

March 1995, Roy Firestone, ESPN:

The six months or so I spent with him at the end were the best six months I've ever spent with another man. He made me understand that life is precious.

February 1993, on a tribute to an obviously fading Valvano before a Duke game at Reynolds Coliseum:

I love that they honored Jimmy. You go through the wars and you compete against each other. I love Jimmy, and I love that North Carolina State honored him today in the proper fashion.

JASON WILLIAMS

Jason Williams was widely considered the premier playmaker in his high school class, and made an early commitment to Duke. He started as a freshman in 2000, helping the Blue Devils to a surprising repeat as ACC champion and the nation's top-ranked team. Williams averaged 14.5 points, second in scoring among freshmen under Krzyzewski only to Johnny Dawkins (18.1 in 1983). The New Jersey product averaged nearly 1.6 assists per turnover, but unofficially had the second-most turnovers in a season (139) in modern ACC history.

Krzyzewski instructing Jason Williams, Duke's most talented point guard since Bobby Hurley.

March 2000:

He never makes an excuse. He takes responsibility. What I didn't know until he played in a game, I didn't know if he had a heart.

June 21, 1999:

He's mature. He's been exposed to a lot. He does have talent, and we have to allow him the opportunity to grow and make mistakes like we did with Tommy and Bobby, and not look at those guys as the finished product but where they started.

JOHN WOODEN

John Wooden coached UCLA to 10 NCAA titles and a dozen Final Fours between 1962 and 1975. Wooden has more championships, more consecutive championships (7), Final Four appearances, Final Four wins (21), and consecutive Final Four appearances (7) than any coach in history. Wooden's Bruins also won an NCAA-record 88 straight games from 1971 through 1974, and counted among their number Lew Alcindor, Bill Walton, Gail Goodrich, and Keith Wilkes.

March 1992, on his program's achievements compared to Wooden's:

I mean, Wooden won ten championships. How can you compare that to going to the Final Four? It's a neat accomplishment, but you certainly can't put it on the same level as winning the whole thing.

Accepting a trophy in 1999 from retired UCLA coach John Wooden.

STEVE WOJCIECHOWSKI

Steve Wojciechowski came to Duke in 1995 with a ready-made nickname and a fiery toughness. The squat, 5–11 Maryland native was sometimes overmatched physically, and only sporadically a threat to score. Yet "Wojo" became a starter at point, as well as a vocal leader and defensive stopper. Wojciechowski paced Duke in assists and steals as an upperclassman, was greeted by barks from students in tribute to his dogged defense, and was named the nation's top defender in 1998, his senior year. Wojo is now a Duke assistant coach.

February 1998, after a win over UNC in which Wojo barely scored yet had Krzyzewski talking of preserving a copy of the boxscore:

It's one of the great one-point performances in the history of the game.

November 1994, on why the freshman started against Connecticut:

Because he's Polish. No, because he plays well. Being Polish didn't hurt him.

April 1998, on watching a video tribute to Wojciechowski following his senior season, Al Featherson, *Durham Herald-Sun*:

I didn't just cry, I sobbed.

LEADERSHIP

I'm a basketball coach, but more than a basketball coach I'm a leader. I had those qualities, then I went to school for leadership, which made me more confident about who I was as a leader, and helped create my leadership style through the successes and failures there in my four years.

GOALS

March 1990:

I'm going to do it the way I think is best to develop these kids each year, being ethical. Ethics has nothing to do with being perfect. Ethics does not equal perfection. Ethics is doing it right, and nothing devious. Ethics is also being sensitive to the other person.

July 1993:

You can't defer if you're the person who's in the leadership position.

November 1980, Dave Fassett, *Duke Chronicle*:

The primary purpose of West Point is to produce leaders, and that's what coaching is all about. Being an officer was good training for coaching, and vice versa. It forces you to mold a group of men with a variety of backgrounds and skills into a cohesive unit.

March 2000:

Leadership is not being a dictator. That is not my form of leadership.

March 2000:

I think leadership is never singular. In a good organization, it's plural.

October 1999, on senior Chris Carrawell and juniors Nate James and Shane Battier, on the eve of a season in which Duke finished 29–5, top-ranked in the polls, and first in the ACC:

I think the success of our team will be based not only on how those three guys play, but lead.

I don't think the leadership of a team comes only from the coach.

COACHING

The rings on Mike Krzyzewski's fingers commemorate his two national titles. Heavy metal. Well into the 1994–95 season he diagrammed plays on the sidelines on a clipboard that said "NCAA Champions 1991." Thirty-four banners celebrating league titles, Final Four appearances, No. 1 rankings, and national championships bristle from the Cameron rafters.

"He has more credibility than pretty much everybody in the business," says 2000–01 senior Shane Battier. "You just look up at the banners, he's pretty much been through every situation."

Krzyzewski is a presence on the sidelines—dark-haired, usually darkly dressed, his visage that of a bird of prey, his emotion often bubbling near the surface. Over the years he's considerably toned

Sometimes Duke huddles are simply opportunities for Krzyzewski to infuse players with his passion.

down his displays of anger, limited by physical problems and informed by self critiques and those of others whom he respects. Ordinarily Krzyzewski perches near the end of Duke's bench closest to the scorer's table, his repertoire of body language readily reflecting his level of approval of what he sees. He arises often to challenge officials or to exhort players. For clearly important games the vehemence increases, both to infuse players with his will, and to bend officials to it.

March 2000, calling himself a "lifer" as a coach:

Because the way we do it, we're not system oriented. You don't just plug something in. It's a huge investment. It's worth it, don't get me wrong. But it's different. That's what I get out of it, but it also takes a lot out of you. There's a lot of stuff that maybe you'd like to do before it's all over. I sound like I'm giving my retirement speech.

June 1999:

I start off every relationship with a kid saying I'm

A brochure from Coach Krzyzewski's early days.

going to tell you the truth. And then we go from there.

December 1989, on the 1986 squad that reached the NCAA title game, losing to Louisville:

That team was truly a basketball team. They just functioned better as a unit than any one of them would have ever functioned as an individual.

December 1992, to his team at practice:

How did you feel when you got a loose ball? The main thing about it is, you feel good about it. That's what the whole fucking game is all about, feeling good about what you're doing.

February 1999, on yelling at officials and taking off his jacket after watching Trajan Langdon get his lip "shattered, really, just shattered" by a Clemson players's elbow:

As soon as I stop being emotional, then someone else should sit here.

November 1994:

If you're a teacher and a coach, you have to have high expectations no matter what group you have.

June 1990, on Dean Smith's thirty-six-year tenure at North Carolina:

I'm not sure anyone will coach for thirty years anymore.

February 1993:

I need some affection back, whether it be someone yelling back at me, holding my arm tight in a huddle, or whatever.

April 7, 1993, on that winter's NCAA loss to California, at a banquet attended while recruiting Allen Iverson:

In the locker room after that game was one of the really great things I've experienced in eighteen years of coaching. Everybody was crying. Everybody. Everybody was hugging. One of the things I'll always remember, I must have hugged Bobby Hurley for a minute. It was over. It wasn't that we lost.

What you do here is not about winning and losing; it's about the bonds you develop. I'm not sure if it's cool to cry. But crying then was good. If you don't have the ability to cry at the end, maybe you missed out on something. Maybe you didn't create that bond.

April 1992, when told Michigan coach Steve Fisher attributed Duke's success to a combination of coaching, talent, and luck:

The proportions are probably 60–30–10. Put them in any order you want.

October 1989:

Sometimes if you're too patient, you're too tolerant. A really, really patient coach isn't necessarily a good coach.

February 1993:

I coach not to win or lose, I coach to have everybody on the same page with heart, mind, and soul. And if it can't happen, then I don't want to coach.

TEAMWORK

December 1996:

I think the trend is for more individualism, and that individualism can show up in "I'm going to concentrate on my game, I'm going to concentrate on my career." Everything I said had to do with "my." There seems to be some of that mentality coming into basketball. "My game, my game." The beauty of the game has always been "our game."

December 1986:
It's easier to have a "we" identity on defense.

February 1988:
The dominant team has to be a team, and because you have to have five, six, eight players playing well, that's not always going to happen.

November 1998:
You don't just be a team. You become a team. Through tough games you find that you need each other.

Coach Krzyzewski deftly varies his emotional and vocal output to meet his players' motivational needs.

THE GAME OF LIFE

I believe in responsibility and discipline. Those are two words that are not running wild in our country. . . . Those two things we've tried to establish, and then a competitive element internally that will help us get out of each other what we need to compete with other people.

GOING PRO

Just down the road from Durham, the University of the North Carolina takes regular if unpredictable hits with players leaving early for professional ball, yet manages to sustain a level of consistent excellence. Starting with Bob McAdoo in 1972, the Tar Heels have seen ten players leave for the pros with eligibility remaining, most notably James Worthy (1982), Michael Jordan (1984), and Vince Carter (1999).

The premature departure of prominent talents helped cost Bobby Cremins his job at Georgia Tech in 2000, and has become relatively commonplace among the college game's elite programs. From 1994 through 1999, sixteen ACC players left early. Until then, just eighteen had left over a 23-year span.

None of the departures were from Duke until the spring of 1999. The issue was hardly raised during the careers of stars like Johnny Dawkins (1983–86), Danny Ferry (1986–89), Christian Laettner (1989–92), and Grant Hill (1991–94), whose retired jerseys hang from the Cameron rafters.

The picture abruptly changed following a 1999 season in which Duke was 37–2, finished atop the polls, won all nineteen ACC games it played, and was upset by Connecticut in the NCAA championship game.

Three players left early. First was national player of the year Elton Brand, doubtless influenced by fresh memories of a foot injury that sidelined him for 15 games in 1998.

Then came fellow sophomore guard William Avery, who met with stinging public disapproval from Krzyzewski. "I'm not in favor of William's decision at this time," the coach said in a press release. "We have done extensive research into the NBA for William and my conclusion was that entering the draft now would not be in his best interests. However, everyone is entitled to make their own decisions . . . "

Elton Brand, the 1999 national player of the year, felt guilty being the first player to decide to leave Duke early, according to Krzyzewski.

Finally, Duke said goodbye to freshman Corey Maggette. Later it was discovered Maggette accepted an illegal financial inducement from an AAU coach during high school, threatening Duke's 1999 runner-up status and NCAA revenue.

Contemplating this changing landscape, Krzyzewski began stocking up on talent long before he finally lost players to the pros. The recruiting class that included Brand, Avery, and Shane Battier was considered among the nation's best, and was followed two years later by another top group—Carlos Boozer, Mike Dunleavy, Nick Horvath, Casey Sanders, and Jason Williams. They signed before Brand and company left, and in 2000 helped spearhead Duke's repeat finish atop the polls and ACC standings.

July 1996:

If you, as a rising senior in high school, feel that you may go pro at the end of your high school career, or at the end of one year in college, for the most part those kids are not going to maximize people, academic, extracurricular skills that could be developed. They have a mindset already. And so the creativity, the imagination, the goal-setting that should run rampant during a youngster's life from sixteen to nineteen, all the dreams are packaged in one setting for kids who, most of them, don't have all the abilities to do that. And I find that sad.

June 1997, considering increased emphasis on pro aspirations at an early age:

To me, the most poignant example I can give of that: When Grant Hill was a senior, no one was asking him whether he would go pro. Now Grant Hill would be asked more whether he's going pro than whether he's going to go to school.

June 1999, on approaching the NBA about having an age minimum for being allowed into the pro ranks, facing the imminent, early loss of three underclassmen:

I really think that the NBA and the players' union would cooperate if they knew who to cooperate with. I think the NCAA is negligent, is what I'm saying. The NCAA is terrific; it needs to change.

In 1972 Hall of Famer Bob McAdoo became the first of many great North Carolina players to turn pro early.

July 1996, on young players discussing their professional aspirations:

What are they supposed to tell people?

Forward James Worthy led North Carolina to the 1982 national title even as Krzyzewski's second Duke squad finished 10-17. He left North Carolina after his junior season and was drafted No. 1 by the Los Angeles Lakers.

If they don't say that, then it's like a knock to their manhood. They have to say I may go. So you create a mindset.

June 1999, on players leaving early:
I would always want a kid to come back and finish his education. I don't know anything that's worth more than your education.

June 1999, on Avery, Brand, and Maggette:
Those kids were exposed to extremes. Over the last two years they've won almost as much as any team, any program in the history of basketball. Sixty-nine wins. In a conference. Come on. They've been exposed to extreme notoriety and success.

June 1999, on completing a college education:
I could never see, for me, what price you pay for not finishing. Just because I'm fifty-two, I know the relationships that are developed. It's an incredible time in your life for growth—personally, academically, everything. I would always want my son to finish.

FISHBOWL

June 1990:

I hate when our fans, when something happens at Carolina or State, they gloat. I hate that. Just like I can't stand it when someone will write a letter to the editor and say, "Well, Duke is bad because Joe Cook flunked."

No, Duke is good because Joe Cook should have flunked. Did Duke do everything to help? Damn right they did! Just like any other school probably did whatever they did.

Duke's Gothic West Campus is the center of university life and site of Cameron Indoor Stadium.

June 1990:

Why shouldn't a kid be allowed to flunk a course in private? I don't like that. They're public figures by default, not by choice, and everyone says they get this and they get that. Baloney. They get robbed of a lot of things that a normal college student gets, and then everyone says we're going to make them a normal college student.

SHAPE OF
THE GAME

Krzyzewski is an outspoken advocate of giving coaches more say in NCAA councils, this during an era when the organization increasingly embraces reforms that limit coaches and move key decision-making away from athletic personnel and into the hands of university presidents. He argues college basketball should have its own governing body or overseeing coordinator to monitor day-to-day operations and plan for the sport's long-range health. He insists his concern is primarily for the welfare of student-athletes, and worries the game's prosperity is taken for granted.

June 1999, on men's basketball needing daily governance and long-range planning:

It should not be a second job. It should be a primary job. Our sport deserves it, and our sport has been hurt by not having that.

It goes against the very structure of the NCAA. The NCAA has never been sport-specific. Its rulebook is all-encompassing. A decision that's made in one sport has to be carried over to another. That's just the way they've run their business. And it should be apparent that the time has come to make a change in that business, especially with this sport that produces over 90 percent of the total revenue of the entire organization.

The demands on any business that would give that much in the running of the business, if you had CEOs and business people analyze it, they'd say, "Come on, this can't work. We have to do something specific here."

It's a change, and change is very slow in the NCAA. But it's needed right now.

October 1999:

In the NBA they market individuals—Grant Hill, Kobe Bryant, Shaquille O'Neal, Tim Duncan, whatever. In college basketball we should not promote individuals, including coaches. We should promote schools and rivalries. They're forever. People, the individual person or coach, is not forever.

That type of promotion would really help. It focuses on—I hate to curse here—school. I'm sorry. It focuses on school. I can't believe I

Krzyzewski preaches worrying about Duke, not the opponent.

was talking about that. School's kind of nice. Since we are NCAA, we should promote school. School. The Michigan-Ohio State football game. The Duke-North Carolina basketball game. Indiana-Kentucky. St. John's-Syracuse. Syracuse-Georgetown. Wow!

January 1993, addressing the NCAA convention on restoring a scholarship and a third, fully paid assistant in an appearance some administrators viewed as presumptuous and a bit comic:

I must say it hurts me when people joke about the numbers of coaches, and to hear laughing and clapping. I implore you to have a better relationship and a better understanding of what's going on with coaches. We are trustworthy. We are teachers. And we're your closest link to why we are here—the student-athlete. If you don't at least listen, that's wrong. You don't have to agree. Just listen. That's all we ask.

July 1991:

The reform isn't in anything that cost money. If it costs money, it's defeated.

August 1992, on reducing scholarships to thirteen for men's basketball:

What are we doing? What the hell are we doing?

January 1992:

I'm very down. There's a closed ear concerning men's basketball. A closed ear. I don't understand it. I absolutely do not understand it. We've been trying to work through proper channels and it hasn't worked at all.

PROGRAM

There's a significant difference between assembling a team and establishing a program—that overarching context within which squads and individual players are molded, bolstered by tradition and, most often, success. Inside a stable system older players pass on advice and standards to newcomers, augmenting and cushioning lessons imparted by coaches. In Duke's case, man-to-man defense and motion offense are given parts of that equation, as are an emphasis on flexibility, playing intelligently with sustained emotion and effort, and communicating on and off the court.

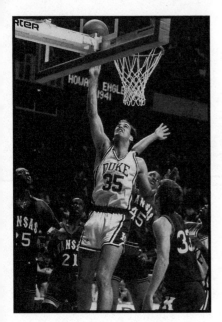

Versatile big man Danny Ferry was the first of several sons of ex-pros to gravitate to Krzyzewski's program.

Krzyzewski's program, bolstered by nineteen McDonald's all-Americans since 1990, is a meritocracy in which the strong survive and prosper, while others either slide to the end of the bench or transfer. An emphasis on developing players' versatility has attracted the sons of coaches and of pro athletes like Bob Ferry (son Danny), Calvin Hill (Grant), Doug Collins (Chris), and Mike Dunleavy (Mike).

By the early 1990s the Duke program ranked among the game's most envied and prestigious. "Everybody hates you because you're Duke," marveled guard Steve Wojciechowski after one game. "Not because you're a bad guy, but because you have Duke across your uniform." When his team beat Duke by 11 points in 1994 and fans stormed the court at Chapel Hill, North Carolina coach Dean Smith offered, "Actually, it was a nice tribute to what the Duke program is."

November 1980, referring to his military background, Dave Fassett, *Duke Chronicle*:

I don't wear fatigues and drive a jeep to work. I have only one rule for my players—don't do anything detrimental to the basketball program.

January 1999:

Every time we play, it's the other team's big game.

June 1987:

I would not want to say that there is a Duke player or a Duke type. We have all different kinds of things. But how they develop and how they leave here, hopefully, recognizes a Duke player as being a good person, a good player who fights you to win and does it in a classy manner. That's how I would like to have our program perceived.

January 1989, David Leon Moore, *USA Today*:

I'm proud of what we're doing here. I'm not saying we're God's gift to education, or better than anybody else. But I think we're doing our job.

March 2000:

Heck, our school has been to more Final Fours than other conferences—conferences!—in the nineties.

WINNING

Krzyzewski has won 571 games in his career against 219 defeats, a .723 winning percentage. His record in two decades at Duke is 498–160, a .757 mark and more victories than any two coaches in school history. His 214 wins in ACC competition (against 108 defeats) and total victories as a conference coach are second only to North Carolina's Dean Smith. His 50 NCAA

Krzyzewski and North Carolina's Dean Smith were mutually respectful, but got under each other's skins.

Tournament wins (against 14 losses) leads active coaches and are second only to Smith all time.

March 1992, on playing to win:

That's a habit. That's a habit that's not based on who you're playing.

March 1989:

I consider myself a teacher, not a basketball coach. If all there was to it was how many games you won, I wouldn't be very happy. That's not what I want to be judged on. I'm no different than the professor in the engineering school. I want my young people to be successes.

February 1993, on winning a national championship:

They don't have to be the most talented team to win. And if we don't win, is that bad? Really, is that bad if we're as good as we can be? As long as we can live with ourselves.

NORTH CAROLINA

North Carolina has been the team to beat for much of the ACC's history. Frank McGuire won a national championship there in 1957, and Dean Smith won two—in 1982 and 1993. Smith also set a remarkable standard of consistent excellence: making the NCAA tournament every season from 1975 through his retirement in 1997; finishing in the league's top three every year since 1965; and winning at least 21 games from 1971 onward. Smith's teams were talented, smart, meticulously prepared, and as relentlessly competitive as their coach.

Smith, who finished with more victories than any coach in Division I history (879), often got under the skin of rival coaches. Krzyzewski, like contemporary Jim Valvano at North Carolina State, arrived when Smith was already at the height of his power, and quickly professed admiration. That's not to say, however, that Smith, through his approach to the game and his comments about Duke, didn't irritate Krzyzewski, at least privately.

Duke's rivalry with North Carolina, once bitter, dates to days

Since Dean Smith retired at UNC in 1997, Krzyzewski and his program have stood alone atop the ACC.

when the private Durham school was named Trinity College. Animosity between players has cooled, but on-court clashes still produce what Krzyzewski called "as intense a ballgame as you can have." Meeting on homecourts located only eleven miles apart, both teams were ranked in the top ten for 21 of their last 48 games. Krzyzewski's record is 20–26 against UNC, 6–2 against Bill Guthridge, who succeeded Smith from 1998-2000.

Unknown:

The only difference between Duke and North Carolina is that Carolina is nine miles away from a great university.

March 2000, addressing Duke students on the eve of Carolina's visit to Durham, Matthijs Schoots, the *Spectator*:

Tomorrow is about the best game every year in college basketball. It can't be the one in Chapel Hill because they don't put their students around the court unless it snows.

April 1993:

Are you kidding? To have the last three national champions in this area is incredible, absolutely incredible. Where else? There's nothing like it.

February 1997, addressing about 1,500 students at Cameron Indoor Stadium the night prior to hosting UNC:

Cheer hard, be innovative, but don't help the enemy. I wouldn't call them any names. Heck, they've got the worst name in the world—Carolina. How can you top that?

TOLERANCE

April 1993:

If I get out of coaching, I would love to get involved in some type of race relations. Basketball is the best example of how people get along. We're all visible. We love each other. We're like brothers. I hate the fact that people can look so incredibly down on someone because of the color of their skin.

April 1993, on arriving at West Point:

I'd never heard of an Episcopalian. It could have been a disease.

April 1993, after several dozen fellow students taunted his daughter— chanting "Go Heels" and shouting "Your dad sucks!"—at the private school she attended:

She was just bawling. She said, "Dad, I don't play." I just wonder in those situations, how the school allows that. I feel bad for (my children). I go to my office. I'm divorced from that. But my kids aren't. They become the focus of that hatred, whatever you call that feeling people have.

March 1994, regarding racism:
I see it with my own daughters—they have none of the prejudices that were prevailing because of lack of interaction that I was exposed to.

MEDIA

Duke locker rooms are favorite media haunts. Colleges allow far less access to players than do the pros, and many schools close their locker rooms entirely, only bringing out select players following a game. Some programs that do open the inner sanctum impose time limits, then kick out reporters.

Under Krzyzewski, Duke's locker room is usually open as long as players care to entertain questions.

The coach, on the other hand, has become less accessible over the course of his tenure. Early on, while somewhat combative with the media, he held weekly press luncheons. He was relatively easy to reach, until the run of Final Fours and championships placed heightened demands on his time. Now he remains professional, if distant, with reporters and has his assistants do the obligatory coach's radio call-in show.

The ACC's senior coach often displays boyish enthusiasm discussing a hard-fought game or superior performance.

January 1990, to ten Duke *Chronicle* reporters invited to come before coaches and team in the locker room following publication of a story rating the basketball squad and players in the student newspaper:

You can interpret it any way you want to because you have freedom of the press. But it is also my freedom of speech to tell you what I think. I think your article, Brent, is full of shit. OK?

You can rip me, praise me, whatever you want, but you guys are really screwing our basketball team and I wanted to tell you that personally. I'm not looking for puff pieces or anything like that, but you're whacked out and you don't appreciate what the fuck is going on and it pisses me off.

I'm just suggesting if you want to appreciate what's going on, get your head out of your ass and start looking for what's actually happening.

June 1998, on media coverage in North Carolina after he criticized the antics of UNC big man Makhtar Ndiaye, who leapt atop a press table, waved a white towel, and thumped his chest in front of the Duke rooting section after the Tar Heels won the 1998 ACC Tournament final:

There's a Carolina bias. There is. But I've lived with it. I don't even think that some of the people know that they have it. But that's why it's laughable to me. It always has been. But it really proved to me that it's true, because for two weeks every letter to the editor (was about that). And the newspapers wanted to print that, that I am like the most terrible guy in the whole world.

COACH K HIMSELF

You're like my wife, asking me about all these hypothetical situations. I'd rather deal with the fact that we are ranked number one. That's where it's at. If we're not number one, then I'll deal with that. I have a big nose. But I don't sit around saying, "I wonder what it would be like without a big nose. I'd like to have a little nose." I don't do things like that. What do you think? Do you think I'd look better with a little nose?

AGE

Born on February 13, 1947, Krzyzewski enjoys being physically active. Until back, ankle, and hip injuries limited his mobility, he frequently jogged and played basketball, racquetball, and tennis. While his hairline has receded, his hair remains quite black.

March 1999, Elizabeth Oliver, *Fifty Plus:*

I've never thought about age, ever. I'm so active and busy, and I feel good emotionally and spiritually. I have passion, a sense of purpose.

March 1999, on Southwest Missouri State players bumping chests with coach Steve Alford:

You know, when you get over fifty, your chest isn't where it used to be.

October 1999, on the start of his twentieth year at Duke, referring to his first head coaching job at age twenty-eight:

It's hard to believe. I guess when you start to be a head coach when you're eighteen, that's what happens. I give credit to the United States Military Academy for having the guts to hire a teenager. It's been great and I've loved it.

BACKGROUND

Michael William Krzyzewski was born in Chicago and raised on the ground floor of a rented house on Cortez Street on the city's South Side. Relatives lived upstairs. "Mick" and his buddies—Moe, Twams, Sel, Stas, Porky, and others—frequented the asphalt playground at nearby Christopher Columbus public school and called themselves the Columbos.

His parents, Bill and Emily Krzyzewski, were immigrants more comfortable speaking Polish, their native language. Both had blue-collar jobs much of their lives. They sent their two sons, Bill and Mike, to Catholic schools. The Krzyzewskis were thrilled when their younger son, a basketball star at Weber High, was offered a scholarship to West Point to play under coach Bobby Knight.

March 1990, discussing communication and honesty:

I can remember growing up and a number of my cousins changed their names. My dad did too, but not legally. My dad used the name Kross. The first part of our name means "cross."

And one of my uncles who was a cop, he used to say, "What's your name?" And I couldn't pronounce it real well—Krzyzewski. He says, "Don't you forget it. I want you to be proud of who you are, your heritage, just like everybody else should be proud. You shouldn't change. Don't change your name."

February 1986:

It's the old thing about growing up in a poor neighborhood. You want to teach your kids to know how to want, to be hungry.

Pictured here in his early days at Duke, Krzyzewski has a knack for keeping his hair black and in almost-perfect place.

February 1983, recalling he wanted to attend college at Wisconsin or Creighton:

When my parents found out I might be able to go to West Point, it was an unbelievable thing. To them, that was the best. They couldn't imagine that their son could go to West Point. In their minds, West Point was for the rich, powerful.

February 1984, on attending West Point, Ron Morris, *Durham Morning Herald*:

But what it teaches you is, one, don't give up. You plan, organize, and be ready to accept criticism. I'm not a real big military man, or anything like that.

FAMILY

Krzyzewski has an older brother, Bill, who still lives in Chicago. Their parents are deceased, Emily Krzyzewski in October 1996 and Bill Krzyzewski, a heavy smoker, in 1969. Krzyzewski married Carol (Mickie) Marsh of Alexandria, Virginia, in 1969, on the day he graduated from West Point. They have three adult daughters—Debbie, Lindy, and Jamie—and a one-year-old grandson, Joey.

Krzyzewski, with wife Mickie, had two young daughters, Debbie and Lindy (in arms), when they took the Duke job.

February 1993, on a motivational harangue delivered to his team following what he called a "horrible" practice:

When I talked about my mom, that's when I started crying. I said that you think I'm going to say, "Yeah, Coach K, now, I'll bet you walked six miles through snow to go to school every day." And, no, I took a bus. I had good clothes. I had enough money. I never knew we were semi-poor, but my mother didn't have crap. She had two dresses in her closet for my whole life. Still does, because her first thing was to think about me and my brother.

March 1989:

You walk into your gym and there's always someone cleaning it. You walk into your office and

112

there's someone changing the light bulbs. I hate when someone looks at people doing those jobs as stupid. My parents are smart. They just didn't have the opportunity. I had the opportunity.

March 1999, Elizabeth Oliver, *Fifty Plus*:
Having daughters has really helped me. They are much more expressive than guys, and it has given me a balance in my male world.

March 1990, on his father:
He was an elevator operator for about twenty-three, twenty-four years and then he opened a very small restaurant in the factory section of Chicago which was mostly breakfast and lunch, I think for factory workers. Then he had that for a few years, and that didn't turn out real well. Then he bought a small neighborhood tavern which he had in the south side of Chicago for a few years, and then he died while he still had the tavern.

March 1990 on the "shock" that his father had numerous health problems:
My dad died twenty-one years ago when I was a senior at West Point. No, he died just before the end of my playing season my senior year, from a cerebral hemorrage. I wasn't always aware of what was going on with him. This was when I was at

West Point and my family didn't tell me a whole lot. They were more, "Don't bother Mike while he's doing that." That's just the way we grew up—don't let him know.

Mike and Mickie Krzyzewski with daughters Lindy (left), Debbie (center with husband Peter Savarino), and Jamie.

March 1999, on his wife and daughters, Ron Green, Jr., *Charlotte Observer*:
I've never had a time when they said, "You love basketball more than me." I wonder how many coaches can say that?

February 1998, after beating UNC, making a comparision to playmaker Steve Wojciechowski, who played a stellar game while scoring a single point:
My daughter Jamie plays point guard at Durham Academy. She's a sophomore. I always tell her, she's too concerned with her shot.

March 1992, after his wife and daughters did the tomahawk chop along with Florida State fans when the Seminoles faced North Carolina in the ACC Tournament:
For this tournament, I don't know what in the hell my family does. They approach this thing like Duke groupies.

PLAYING CAREER

Krzyzewski, a guard, lettered at Army from 1967 through 1969. During his career the Cadets were 51–23, twice led the nation in scoring defense, and twice reached the NIT, then a prestigious achievement. Krzyzewski, a defensive specialist and team captain as a senior, hit 45.7 percent from the floor, a handsome 75.9 percent at the foul line, and averaged 6.2 points.

"Mike was a terrific basketball player," Bob Knight, his coach at Army, said in 1987. "I admired how hard he played. Mike was a great defensive player, the best on the team. I though he was the heart and soul of what the team got accomplished."

Dave Bliss, current head coach at Baylor, was an assistant at Army when Krzyzewski played. Thirty years later, he vividly recalled an incident involving Krzyzewski in a 1968 game against Bradley at Lexington in the Kentucky Invitational.

"Mike was one of the toughest players," Bliss said. "There was a loose ball, and his eye was gouged. He could hardly see out of it. It was tearing up. But he went to the line and made both free throws."

February 1986:

I think playing up at Army developed mental toughness, playing for Coach Knight.

March 1987:

It was my senior year and we were playing South

Once so close they kept in regular touch by phone, Krzyzewski and his mentor, Bob Knight (left), are no longer on speaking terms.

Carolina. Only two guys were designated shooters on the team. We're in there and Knight says to me, "You're not allowed to shoot." That was nothing new to me.

He said, "You take a shot and I will break your arm." So, I had this opening—I mean, I was really open—and I went up to the foul line, but I stopped right there. As I cocked my shooting arm, my whole life passed before me.

I passed off. We won. So, it worked.

Built with tobacco money on the edge of a late nineteenth-century boomtown in north central North Carolina, Duke University once was a regional school affiliated with the Methodist church. Duke began playing men's basketball in 1906, and first became a national power under Vic Bubas during the 1960s. The private school has 6,207 undergraduates, these days from all over the world, having widened its horizons in competition with Ivy League universities. Tuition, fees, room and board are around $30,000 annually.

Duke's alumni base and student body are dwarfed by its nearest ACC neighbors, public universities North Carolina, undergrad enrollment 15,700, and N.C. State, 18,700. Between them the three "Research Triangle" schools are responsible for all seven NCAA titles won by ACC teams, as well as twenty-eight of thirty-two Final Four berths secured by league members since 1954.

November 1980, Dave Fassett, *Duke Chronicle:*

Sometimes you walk into a place and it just feels right. That's the type of feeling I had about Duke. I had kind of a gut feeling that I would get the job, and I can't envision myself leaving Duke voluntarily.

TV's Dick Vitale routinely raves about Krzyzewski and Cameron, where fans treat him like royalty.

July 1996, on the constant intensity of the rivalry with UNC:

There's no place like here. Good or bad.

October 1991, on the academics being tougher at a state university:

Hey, most kids graduate from our school. They're admitted to graduate.

January 1988, Jerry Lindquist, *Richmond Times-Dispatch:*

The people at Duke are not what I call idol worshippers. They respect you for a job well done, but they're not going to build you a statue. That's good. Why should anybody who's coaching a sport have that?

1989, asked about rumors he'd replace Eddie Sutton as Kentucky's head coach:

I have Duke tattooed on a part of my body I can't show you.

CAMERON INDOOR STADIUM

Cameron Indoor Stadium, designed by an African-American architect in Philadelphia and named for former Duke coach and athletic director Eddie Cameron, opened in January 1940 on the edge of Duke's Gothic West Campus. When built, the stone-faced rectangle was the largest arena south of Philly's Palestra. Today the building seats 9,314, or rather crams that many people into seats and aisles, and is dwarfed by most arenas serving comparably popular programs.

Students ring the court, usually standing throughout a game. Stray birds cavort among rafters where thirty-four men's basketball banners hang in celebration of championships, No.1 poll finishes, and Final Four berths. Even with hinged windows upstairs that let in sunlight and fresh air, January nights can be steamy in Cameron.

Duke students are notorious for their cheering. Some messages are clever, and remarkably attuned to the action or to opponents' offcourt woes. Chants often aim to taunt, and occasionally are abusive. Especially prevalent these days are male body-painting and cheers like "Whiny Bitch!" and, in honor of defensive whiz Shane Battier, "Who's Your Daddy? Battier!"

The students tend to revel in their cleverness and to pose for TV cameras, but do strive to lend the Blue Devils verbal and emotional support. Distracting stratagems assault visitors toeing the foul line or trying to run down the clock, and every game is occasion for at least one round of chanting "Go to hell, Carolina!" that ends with a hearty chorus of "Eat Shit!"

Following a 1994 visit, Temple's crusty John Chaney observed of Cameron and Mike Krzyzewski: "This is perhaps one of the finest basketball arenas that you can think of, and this guy's probably one of the few guys I would swap jobs with."

Cameron is awash in sound from the opening tap, and can grow so loud spectators must shout to be heard by neighbors, leaving ears vibrating long after the game. With its brass rails, hard-backed seats, wooden bleachers, intimate air, and sense of suspended time, Krzyzewski rightly calls Cameron "just a neat atmosphere for college basketball."

The game atmosphere at Cameron Indoor Stadium, opened in 1940, is hot, loud, intimate, and intense.

March 1999:

This place has a way of keeping not just ghosts but—I don't know, birds too, and squirrels—it keeps feelings in here. I don't know, it's a building of enormous feeling.

February 1988, after a 101–63 win over Clemson:

We have something very special here at Duke, and that's the intimacy that has developed between the students and their team. I'm glad the Duke administration always looks at it that the Duke students get the best seats.

EARLY

Krzyzewski took over at Duke in March 1980. He followed a successful older coach, Bill Foster, whose Blue Devils played for the national title in 1978 and reached the Sweet 16 in 1980. Krzyzewski was Duke's head fourth coach in nine years, arriving with a modest reputation, a 9–17 record at Army the previous season, and a name few could pronounce. He quickly encountered friction with holdover players. His second and third teams lost 17 games each, sparking considerable grumbling among fans and media members. At times Krzyzewski openly bristled at inquiries about his strategic choices, particularly an insistence on employing man-to-man defense at virtually all costs.

May 1980, to a group of students at a Duke dorm shortly after being hired, Art Chansky, *Durham Morning Herald*:

If any of you have a 6–9 neighbor who can play, call the basketball office.

June 1992:

When we were 11–17, I was thinking of working for the *News and Observer*. Not as a reporter.

PROFANITY

Krzyzewski can curse vigorously, though usually it's confined to private team settings—the locker room, practice, huddles. The words do also spill out during interviews and when Krzyzewski addresses officials during games. Such public airings of verbal dirty laundry cause consternation among some Duke folks, and gleeful disdain among Tar Heel faithful accustomed to decades of expletive-deleted comportment by Dean Smith and Bill Guthridge, his successor.

June 1990, on the use of expletives

There's a place for that, if the group you're saying it to is accustomed to that. In other words to get a point across, like in the military. If we're on the front lines I'm saying you'd better get your ass moving, buddy. Now I'm not going to say that in church, but if that's what a person is accustomed to.

November 1995:
I used to say bullshit and now I say bullcrap. I've done a lot of soul-searching during my time off.

March 1992, on yelling at players:
They're men. There's not enough time to say excuse me. I get in their faces. But I also pat them on the back.

INDEBTED TO THE GAME

July 1991, mentioning the contributions of Fred Taylor (Ohio State), Pete Newell (California), and Hank Iba (Oklahoma A&M/State):
My feeling is, the game is going to be there whether Mike Krzyzewski or Bob Knight or Dean Smith or John Thompson or whoever leave the game. You're judged by the state you leave the game. The game will be there. No one is bigger than the game.

July 1991, on contributions to the game by coaches in the form of hosting clinics, coaching all-star teams, serving on NCAA committees, and the like:

There are some guys who don't do anything, nothing, which I think sucks.

September 1999:

I love the game and it's been great to me. It's been unbelievably great to me. I hate when people say the game owes them something. We owe the game.

Hugging Chris Carrawell, 2000 ACC player of the year, as he came to the bench following his final home game.

CHRONOLOGY:

DUKE THROUGH THE KRZYZEWSKI YEARS

1981
17-13 overall, 6-8 ACC regular season, tied for fifth.
Postseason: NIT, lost in third round, 81-69 to Purdue.

1982
10-17 overall, 4-10 ACC regular season, tied for sixth.
Postseason: None.

1983
11-17 overall, 3-11 ACC regular season, seventh.
Postseason: None.

1984
24-10 overall, 7-7 ACC regular season, tied for third, lost in
ACC Tournament final.
Postseason: NCAA, lost in opening game, 80-78 to Washington.
Krzyzewski voted ACC coach of the year.

1985
23-8 overall, 8-6 ACC regular season, tied for fourth.
Postseason: NCAA, lost in second round, 74-73 to Boston
College.

1986
37-3 overall, 12-2 ACC regular season, first, won ACC
Tournament.
Postseason: NCAA, lost in national championship game, 72-69
to Louisville.
Krzyzewski chosen UPI national coach of the year.

1987
24-9 overall, 9-5 ACC regular season, third.
Postseason: NCAA, lost in Sweet 16, 88-82 to Indiana.

1988
28-7 overall, 9-5 ACC regular season, third, won ACC Tournament.
Postseason: NCAA, lost in Final Four, 66-59 to Kansas.

1989
28-8 overall, 9-5 ACC regular season, tied for second, lost in ACC Tournament final.
Postseason: NCAA, lost in Final Four, 95-78 to Seton Hall.
Krzyzewski picked as Naismith national coach of the year.

1990
29-9 overall, 9-5 ACC regular season, second.
Postseason: NCAA, lost in national championship game, 103-73 to UNLV.

1991
32-7 overall, 11-3 ACC regular season, first, lost in ACC Tournament final.
Postseason: NCAA, won title, defeated Kansas in national championship game, 72-65.
Krzyzewski selected NABC national coach of the year.

1992
34-2 overall, 14-2 ACC regular season, first, won ACC Tournament.
Postseason: NCAA, won title, defeated Michigan in national championship game, 71-51.
Krzyzewski voted Naismith and Sporting News national coach of the year.

1993
24-8 overall, 10-6 ACC regular season, tied for third.
Postseason: NCAA, lost in second round, 82-77 to California.

1994

28–6 overall, 12–4 ACC regular season, first.
Postseason: NCAA, lost in national championship game, 76–72 to Arkansas.

1995

13–18 overall, 2–14 ACC regular season, ninth.
Postseason: None.

1996

18–13 overall, 8–8 ACC regular season, tied for fourth.
Postseason: NCAA, lost in first round, 75–60 to Eastern Michigan.

1997

24–9 overall, 12–4 ACC regular season, first.
Postseason: NCAA, lost in second round, 98–87 to Providence.
Krzyzewski chosen Basketball Times national coach of the year.

1998

32–4 overall, 15–1 ACC regular season, first, lost in ACC Tournament final.
Postseason: NCAA, lost in regional final, 86–84 to Kentucky.

1999

37–2 overall, 16–0 ACC regular season, first,
won ACC Tournament.
Postseason: NCAA, lost in national title game,
77–74 to Connecticut.

2000

29–5 overall, 15–1 ACC regular season, first, won
ACC Tournament.
Postseason: NCAA, lost in Sweet 16, 87–78 to Florida.
Krzyzewski ACC coach of the year for fifth time.

THE NUMBERS

.857 winning percentage at Cameron Indoor Stadium
.781 NCAA Tournament winning percentage
.757 winning percentage at Duke (498-160)
.723 career winning percentage at Duke and Army
571 career wins in 25 years as head coach (219 losses)
95 consecutive non-conference home wins (1983-96)
50 NCAA wins
28 consecutive ACC wins
16 NCAA Tournament appearances
15 20-win seasons
11 consecutive NCAA appearances
8 Final Four appearances
8 first place finishes in ACC
6 Appearances in national championship game
5 ACC Tournament titles
5 30-win seasons
5 seasons named national coach of the year
5 ACC coach of the year awards
5 straight Final Four berths
4 times ranked No.1 in final national polls
2 NCAA titles

THE EARLY YEARS

February 13, 1947: Michael William Krzyzewski born in Chicago, Illinois.

1965: Graduated from Weber High School, Chicago.

1967–69: Played for Bob Knight at U.S. Military Academy.

1969: Coached post team to 5th Army championship at Fort Carson, Colorado.

1975: Season as graduate assistant to Knight at Indiana.

1976: First season as head coach at U.S. Military Academy.

1977: First 20–win season.

1978: First postseason appearance, in NIT.

March 18, 1980: Introduced as 19th head coach at Duke.